Vietnam:
Friendships and Kindness in the Midst of War

Qui Nhon USO 69-71

Bette Newton Gregory

DEDICATION

Dedicated to my mother Violet, my husband Richard, and all those who provide a safe caring place we call "Home". It's not a physical location, but a tender feeling carried in the heart, giving us courage when we must be apart from those we love. In Nam we called it "back in the world"...

AUTHOR'S NOTE

This memoir is a work of non-fiction. The letters included in this memoir remain in their original form except in rare instances where names and details have been slightly altered or omitted in consideration of privacy issues.

ACKNOWLEDGMENTS

I wish to give special thanks to the following friends whose lives have been directly affected in various ways by the military conflict in Vietnam. Sharing my story is a way of saying how much I appreciate each of them and the role they played either directly or indirectly in being of service to our country.

PAT DOLAN: As a nurse, Pat, worked in a hospital that cared for wounded Vietnam Veterans in the U.S. as they returned from the war. I met her toward the completion of writing this memoir and asked if she would read the manuscript and share her thoughts since her experiences were very different from mine. As a result I have included her candid questions with my answers following some in-depth reflection from us both.

JOHN DONALDSON: My cousin, John, mentioned in the letters, served as a Marine in Da Nang, Viet Nam in the mid 1960's.

NANCY DUDGEON: Friend since grade school in Seattle, Washington, and wife of Darrell who served in Qui Nhon from 1965-1966.

RICHARD GREGORY: My husband of nearly thirty years who served honorably in the Marine Corps Reserves during the Vietnam era. I extend to Richard my heartfelt thanks for the many hours he gave of his talents and patience to assist with this project.

CHAPLAIN ROY MATHIS: Chaplain of 4th Battalion, 503rd Infantry, 173rd Airborne Brigade, stationed at LZ English outside Qui Nhon, Vietnam from 1969-1970. His book "It Was A Long Way From Home & A Long Time Ago But God Was There" was taken from his journal written during the war at the same time I was writing home to my family. It was his efforts that assisted the Qui Nhon USO staff in visiting units in the field.

MARY MCGLASSON: Friend of forty-six years, Director of Qui Nhon, Vietnam USO and Hanau, Germany USO in addition to other USO assignments.

KATHLEEN MILLER: A friend of recent years who participated in early protests of the war in Vietnam, but wholeheartedly gave her suggestions and encouragement for the writing of this memoir.

TERRY PHILLIPS: Friend of forty-one years, former Red Cross "Donut Dolly" in Vietnam, and USO staff member in Udorn, Thailand and Hanau, Germany.

THOMAS G. SELBY: Friend and spiritual teacher, retired therapist, and Marine Corps veteran of the 9th Marine Reg. 3rd Div. prior to the war in Vietnam, whose enthusiastic support helped see this book reach completion.

To others who gave helpful input to the manuscript, I am deeply grateful.

FOREWORD

This is a story that occurs in the midst of the Vietnam War. It is unlike other stories of war that most of us are used to reading. Bette Newton Gregory is a civilian veteran of that war. She served as Associate Director of the USO Center in Qui Nhon, Vietnam from 1969-1971. Anyone who served in Vietnam during that time was vulnerable to all of the tragedies that can, and do, occur in a war zone. It is natural for anyone to experience anxiety, fear, and sometimes even terror but as you read the letters contained in this book, written by Bette to her family, you may well ask "How can it be that she sounds so joyful?" Well, you would have to know Bette! And the readers of this book are given the opportunity to know her.

I have had the privilege to know Bette for many years, and I assure you, she is not a fictional person. Bette was a light that shone during some of the darkest days of the Vietnam War. The empathy and exuberance that you will experience through her letters was the light of life and hope that she shared with many GI's with whom she served. She exhibited an everyday sanity amidst the insanity that shrouds those who participate in the fog of war. GIs who returned home, as well as those who did not, were never really away from home…if they had the benefit of knowing Bette, who embodied the comfort and caring of "home" to GIs who knew her.

I know Bette would be the first to say that she was just one worker among many. All of the brave and caring civilians who served with the USO during the war deserve recognition and gratitude. I know that not every person who served in Vietnam, military and civilian, experienced the war as Bette did. Her story, however, is one of many that didn't get recorded and shared, until now. In fact, she is like many soldiers returning from any war who haven't talked about the friendships forged and kindnesses extended during their time in what most of us might consider "hell".

To single Bette out is simply to recognize and honor the unique qualities that she embodies and extended. Frightened, confused and despondent soldiers were "home" when in the presence and care of Bette. What a beautiful gift to give and to receive!

Thank you, Bette, and all the USO workers that she represents, for being the bridge of love and kindness to our men and women during a time of our absence.   Thomas G. Selby - Albuquerque, NM

PREFACE

In 2014, while rummaging through the closet, I came across two old shoeboxes. When I opened them, out flew forty-four years of memories. The boxes contained ninety letters I wrote home from Vietnam that mom had neatly numbered, filed, and tucked away.

As I read each letter, emotions that surfaced were not what one would expect from a wartime experience, even though I was a civilian and not involved in direct combat. The happy times from that tragic war were due in large part to making wonderful new friendships, having the opportunity to travel, learning about different cultures, and being able to share it all with my family back home. In addition were the unparalleled rewards of the job itself.

A friend who had been a nurse caring for returning Vietnam veterans, and who had also been a protestor of the war, recently asked me, "How could you find joy in the midst of so much trauma? Were you that shielded from the war? Did you not feel the suffering of these men or your own pain?" My hope is the answer can be found in this memoir, scattered throughout the rich complexity of those eighteen months.

Even now certain events trigger flashbacks to that time. The most frequent is when I hear the sound overhead of a UH-1 Huey Helicopter. The USO, where I served as Associate Director, was located on a U.S. Army airfield in Qui Nhon. Nearby was the 67th Evacuation Hospital. Every day, and throughout each day, we heard choppers coming and going. Some were on missions of mercy bringing wounded to the hospital. Others were transporting troops, bringing them from the field for a day of Rest and Recuperation (R&R) at Red Beach or to the USO Center's Snack Bar and a variety of services. The distinctive sound of a Huey is also a reminder of jumping on board a chopper with a duffle bag full of gifts that my co-workers and I took to troops in the field. This is just one example of a wide range of feelings, including happiness and sadness, as a response to that one sound. I'm often reminded of those suffering from PTSD who continue battling an inner war re-ignited by similar sights and sounds. It's therefore been a challenge remaining sensitive to others still living with negative consequences of war, while at the same time, giving myself permission to share a personal story mostly positive in nature.

After reading the letters, I decided to do an internet search, to see if I could learn the whereabouts of anyone I knew in Nam. The first name I entered was that of Chaplain Roy Mathis. Chaplain Mathis was a good friend to all the staff at the USO in Qui Nhon. He, in fact, had arranged most of our visits to units in the field. He served as chaplain to the 173rd Airborne Brigade. It came as a pleasant surprise to find that while I was constantly writing letters home to my mom, he was journaling daily events from where he was stationed at Brigade Headquarters about 60 miles north. I was also delighted to read an article about a book he had written called "It Was A Long Way From Home And A Long Time Ago But God Was There!" After contacting Chaplain Mathis and ordering his book, he encouraged me to write about my own tour in Nam with the USO. I think we both realized that my account would be quite different from his even though we often wrote about the very same events. After all, I was a single twenty-seven year old civilian and he was a happily married military chaplain stationed in the middle of a fierce field of battle. It was clear my story, if written, would be coming from quite a different perspective.

So, here we are, a couple of years later, after picking up the pen and putting it down, vowing numerous times to never write another line. I must say, however, that this entire process of writing a memoir has brought about some amazing adventures of its own. Longtime friends are even closer now after we are finally able to talk about our feelings and how nobody wanted to discuss the war when we got home.

INTRODUCTION

In 1969 I made the decision to accept an assignment with the USO. At that time women were being hired to work in seventeen USO Centers scattered across South Vietnam. The idea was to provide the United States military with a touch of home, during an unpopular war, when men were subjected to the draft. Upon reflection, I can see how that choice to leave a stressful work environment became a somewhat daring leap of self-discovery. I had been blessed with an ordinary life that was about to become extraordinary.

Just before the outbreak of WWII, Franklin D. Roosevelt mobilized six agencies to support various needs of the growing U.S. military. Those agencies were: Salvation Army, YMCA, YWCA, National Catholic Community Services and the National Jewish Welfare Board. As a result a new program was formed named United Service Organization or more commonly the "USO". Many fondly remember USO sponsored dances for the troops prior to their shipping out to fight in Europe and the South Pacific. Over the years well-known entertainers like Bob Hope and Martha Raye plus numerous others, spent countless hours and many tours cheering up the military around the world with the USO. Martha Raye visited bases, field units, and hospitals throughout Vietnam for years and was injured twice.

There were no welcoming parades for the military or civilians returning home from the Vietnam War. From anti-war protestors, those who dodged the draft and fled to Canada, veteran's suffering PTSD, to a war weary public, few were interested in discussing what took place in S.E. Asia. It's no wonder many have remained silent over the years.

Looking back at my family history it's clear, I must have inherited a "gypsy spirit" from both sides of the family.

My father, Cly Cleburn Newton, along with his stepfather, William Newton (Honest Bill), were proprietors of several well known circus's in the United States from 1917 through 1937.

Violet Moore, the dearest mother a girl could have, met my dad in her hometown of Ada, Oklahoma, where the circus wintered at the local fairgrounds. Their first date was going for a horseback ride on Christmas Day. I think one look at my handsome father riding his black stallion, was enough for mom to marry this circus owner and join him in traveling back and forth across the country. This lifestyle must have been quite a challenge for mom, a small town teacher who loved books, poetry and playing the piano.

Even my maternal grandmother, Iola Moore, (otherwise know as Mamoo), enjoyed a somewhat unusual life. In the early 1900's in Ada, she and my grandfather owned and ran a popular boarding house. After his passing, she made her way to California, and for a year worked in the household of actor, Fred MacMurray. Then, during World War II the family including my aunt, uncle and their one year old son, migrated to Seattle, Washington where I was born in 1942. Mom's sister, Bid, and her husband, Dick Donaldson, had moved to Seattle so he could work in the naval shipyard. My childhood was therefore spent within an extended family when they jointly bought a home, and I grew up with my two cousins Dick and John. Mamoo, who also moved to Seattle, was hired to supervise the household staff for a wealthy family who owned a mansion on Lake Washington.

In 1959, the entire family moved back to Oklahoma, this time to Oklahoma City. Preferring a small town atmosphere, I spent four years at East Central State College in Ada, from which I graduated. Inspired by President John F. Kennedy's appeal for everyone to get involved and do something for the country, I joined the newly formed Volunteers in Service to America (VISTA) program, and spent a year in the desert of Arizona working with Hispanic families.

Following that year, I moved back with my family taking a position as residential advisor at the Job Corps Center for Women in Guthrie, Oklahoma. I worked there until my doctor confirmed that I was totally "burned out". It was at that time someone suggested I write to the national office of the USO to inquire about any job openings. Four months later, I found myself in Southeast Asia working as Associate Director of the Qui Nhon USO.

QUESTIONS and ANSWERS

As I came toward the end of writing this memoir, one of those wonderful incidents of serendipity occurred. After months of encouragement from my friend, Tom Selby, to proceed with this project, I met his wife, Pat Dolan. Tom kept telling me that my participation was an aspect of the war that few people knew about. As a Marine Corps veteran, minister and recently-retired therapist, he said there is still so much healing that needs to occur in our country in regard to the war in Vietnam. What he didn't mention was his wife, Pat, had been a nurse working in a hospital that cared for wounded veterans returning from Vietnam. She was also an avid protestor against the war. Learning of her background, I asked if she would read my manuscript and give her honest reaction. She not only said yes but, after reading the draft, responded with a number of candid questions. This prompted me to explore thoughts I had previously never asked myself, most likely because the time just hadn't been right. As a result, it was not only enlightening for both of us, but uncovered some unexpected reactions as well.

Soon after visiting with Pat, I phoned Terry Phillips, my friend of over forty years, and asked if she would add some of her own thoughts. Terry and I didn't know each other in Vietnam even though we were both working there at the same time. While I remained in Qui Nhon during my eighteen-month tour, Terry worked with the Red Cross as a "Donut Dolly" in several different locations. She and I became aware of the fact that over all these years, the two of us had not discussed the details of our tours in Vietnam with each other or anyone else.

Pondering the questions Pat had raised, Terry had the following realization: "My life journey before going to Vietnam felt like I had only been heading "north". When I arrived overseas, I realized there was also "south". As time passed, I looked further and begin discovering "east" and "west". Allowing myself to open up to 360 degrees, I began to see things differently. I knew there was more to me and the world than I had ever imagined." Terry added that before going overseas she felt invisible throughout her college years. Her motives in accepting an assignment with the Red Cross included a desire to connect more with life and discover new things about herself. In the beginning it was not about altruism, "it was about me" she said. After while there was a shift. "I began caring as much about the troops as I did about myself." They all had become, "my guys". "It was so unreal, like a dream or being on a movie set. I couldn't believe I was actually standing there watching napalm being dropped on people."

Now I know why it has taken me several years of struggle to write this memoir. It wouldn't have been complete without including the heart-felt insights of these two amazing women. Our conversations were most likely similar to the unspoken thoughts and feelings of numerous others who have not yet shared their own experiences surrounding issues of war.

Pat's questions included below, can be read prior to reading the letters, during the letter reading, or at the end of the book. Dates following each question pertain to the specific letter Pat was addressing.

HOW COULD ANYONE FIND JOY IN THE MIDST OF SO MUCH TRAUMA? WERE YOU THAT SHIELDED FROM THE WAR? DID YOU NOT FEEL THE SUFFERING OF THESE MEN OR YOUR OWN PAIN?

If I had allowed myself to be overwhelmed by all the suffering, I couldn't have done my job. As much as I have always had tremendous respect for men and women who care for the sick and wounded, being in the medical field was clearly not my calling. Rather than focusing on that as a weakness, I decided I would find a field where I could explore my strengths.

Upon arrival in Vietnam I was immediately surrounded by hard-working caring individuals (civilian and military) who were doing the best they could under very challenging circumstances. The military draft had imposed difficult choices upon people who were just going about their lives. Many, even those opposed to the war, were suddenly thrust into a foreign country, given a weapon, and told to get out there and kill the enemy (once you can determine who that enemy is).

All I knew about the war in 1969 was that the French had come and gone, now the United States was involved, and there was concern about a "domino effect" implying that the communists were busy grabbing up land and they must be stopped. There was so much upheaval in the "60's" and everyone in the U.S. was affected. I was politically very naive and hadn't formulated an opinion about the war. Looking back, I see how that was an advantage because it allowed me to serve the troops regardless of their political and personal viewpoints. I saw my role as bringing a feeling of "home" and providing brief moments away from the conflict. Our job at the USO Center was not to entertain, heal, or engage in deep philosophical or political issues. It was merely to "show up" and be ourselves.

It's true, while I was often enjoying the extraordinary adventure I found myself in, I knew there was agonizing suffering occurring in every direction. Acknowledging those contrasts, I try to remember that my intention was to care deeply for those who were hurting and do what I could to soften their emotional distress.

Fortunately my upbringing allowed me to feel comfortable whether I was visiting with a young private, dining with an officer, getting acquainted with our Vietnamese staff, or learning about the orphanage from a French Catholic nun. In addition to meeting so many fascinating people, I had the pleasure of sharing it all with my family who let me know how much they enjoyed hearing from me. Mom had always enjoyed good food so I was sure to include the details of many meals. I was also aware how much mom and my aunt enjoyed going on shopping trips for the clothes I needed. I made sure they knew the cologne and mini skirts they sent, along with homemade cookies, plus a smile from me, had the potential of truly brightening up someone's day. We all reaped great rewards from such simple acts.

Long before going to Vietnam I developed coping skills and found ways to shield myself from people in distress. But as the letters home point out, there were occasions when I simply went "numb". The ability to ease pain with joy from wonderful relationships was a gift handed down from my mother. She had such quiet, deep faith and, although I'm sure she didn't fully understand all the decisions I made in life, she nevertheless gave support and encouragement for me to follow my own path.

PLEASE DEFINE "LRRP" AND WHAT WAS IT LIKE WHEN YOU WENT ON VISITS TO THE FIELD?
(August 28, 1969)

LRRP "Long Range Reconnaissance Patrol" meals were freeze-dried, vacuum packed and much lighter than "C" rations. A canteen cup of water could be boiled and poured over it for a hot meal.

One of the most frequent pictures I carry in my mind regarding an experience in the field, was lifting off in a helicopter one day following a cook-out. I don't recall anything that set it apart from other visits except that, as I recall, we had landed in more of a jungle setting than on a hilltop or cleared area. Unlike providing planned activities like the Red Cross Donut Dollies, USO staff didn't wear uniforms and had no organized program during field visits, other than bringing food and distributing mail bags of gifts sent from people back in the states. This provided a relaxed environment in which we could simply mix and visit with the troops.

We knew this unit, like most, was experiencing constant life-threatening missions. I'll never forget how it felt when the cook-out was over and we looked down from the safety of our chopper as this brave group of GI's quietly looked up and waved good-bye.

HOW DID YOU FEEL SEEING THE POW's?
(September 10, 1969)

I had difficulty viewing prisoners as the "enemy" since my encounters with them were in a hospital setting where they looked young, lonely and afraid. One day on a hospital visit, I was feeding ice cream to a Vietnamese patient at the 67th Evac when I glanced over and saw a military guard sitting nearby. It wasn't until then that I realized the patient I was feeding was Viet Cong. In the so-called "fog of war", it can be challenging to make distinctions and judgments. I began to understand why people used the phrase "situation ethics'. For example, our Vietnamese staff were wonderful to me, even when I was supposed to search them as they left the USO at the end of the day. I developed great respect for them, while at the same time knowing the VC might be a child selling trinkets on the beach, hiding a hand grenade. GI's had been killed making the mistake of forgetting that reality.

WHAT A JUXTAPOSITION, i.e., "HAVING A BALL" DURING THE VIETNAM WAR! IN FACT, SO FAR, YOUR WHOLE EXPERIENCE IS A JUXTAPOSITION TO THE HORRORS OF WAR
(October 1, 1969)

Perhaps the pictures included in the memoir will help describe my experience. The scenes tell their own stories of how a semblance of normality continued in the midst of an insane situation. This took place without actually saying more than how good hot food tasted at a cookout. In this particular letter I mention how sweet the Cobra pilots were to me, that ten GI's came to show a good time to little orphans and I got to be with some guys on their day of R&R at Red Beach. One of the strongest reactions my husband felt in reading the letters was how the very presence of American women helped remind the men of their own gentle humanity and gave them an outlet to express it in a variety of ways. It is a testament that even brief encounters we have with each other are worthy of our full attention and reverence.

WHAT IS DEROS? (December 27,1969)
Date of expected return from overseas to the states.

YOU FACED DEATH, AND LOSS, AND PAIN. WHAT DID YOU FEEL THEN AND NOW LOOKING BACK? (JANUARY 9, 1970, also known as "BLACK FRIDAY").

I know there were times when I became numb to events like visits to hospital wards, seeing cribs in the orphanage holding three or four infants, and watching a drowned soldier wash up on a sandy beach. I'm also aware that I reassured my family back home that I was happy and not to worry. I could do that because of the strength of their faith and character, plus the confidence they had that I was joyfully living the life I had chosen. The incident of Black Friday was felt on a particularly personal level in several ways. First, because we knew some of those who were killed or wounded, and secondly, because only one day separated Mary and I from being present at LZ North English when the attack occurred. Immediately upon learning what happened, there wasn't much time to get in touch with our feelings because we spent hours visiting GI's in the hospital.

I can only ask, " How do all of us feel about the circumstances of any war?" There is sadness, anger, confusion, and frustration that people of the world have not yet found a way to handle differences without killing each other.

WHAT KINDS OF THINGS DID YOU TALK ABOUT WITH THE GI's? (January 24, 1970)

Quite honestly, I don't remember and, because I don't recall, my guess is that subjects discussed were often not very deep. Topics might include looking forward to an R&R and occasionally reminiscing about their families. I'm sure it was more comfortable not discussing the war considering the settings we were in. Sometimes living in a war zone feels like you are a world apart from the rest of humanity. That is why returning home can be quite a social and cultural shock, not to mention the difficult transition for those who are wounded. I do remember one of the happier ways the men managed to cope was through their use of humor. Years later, watching television episodes of MASH and China Beach, I would get emotional being reminded of the docs laughing, telling jokes and listening to the radio, while at the same time performing surgery.

WHAT WAS THIS MORTAR ATTACK LIKE FOR YOU AND MARY? (April 1st 1970)

I give a lot of credit to my friend, Mary McGlasson, for being a mentor to me on many occasions. This was one example. She is nearly ten years older than I, and a model of inner strength, intelligence and getting important things done. During the mortar attack she exuded a calmness I'm sure influenced my response, so, when things quieted down we simply got up off the floor and walked outside to watch the sky light up. After seeing what the troops faced every day, it certainly didn't call for any drama from us.

HOW DID YOUR VIETNAM EXPERIENCE CHANGE YOU?
(November 16, 1970)

I find it very difficult to look back at those extraordinary eighteen months and say how I am affected today because of what happened then. What I do know is what a deep "heart connection" I feel about that war and those who participated in any capacity. Today it is common to see a Vietnam Veteran proudly wearing a cap signifying his military service. On several occasions I have been tempted to walk up and introduce myself thanking him for his service, only to find I'm too emotional to speak. What that means, I'm not really sure. Any unconscious healing I may require is more likely to be for our human family in general. That is evidenced by the fact that I have a lump in my throat just watching the morning news. Some of my friends have stopped watching what is called the "news" for that and other reasons, but I still have a strong need to stay connected to the world outside my door even with all its ups and downs. I study and appreciate teachings of non-judgment, non-resistance, loving kindness and forgiveness, knowing I have been guided by a "Higher Power" and "Grand Mystery." I've also been truly blessed having enjoyed the unconditional love of my beautiful mother, who encouraged me through the myriad changes and unconventional paths I chose over the years.

"THE LETTERS"

The heart of this memoir is the letters I wrote home to my mother, aunt, uncle, and grandmother. Forty years later I found these letters in a shoe box my mother kept for me. Hastily written during very busy days, they reflect scattered thoughts and a roller coaster of conflicted emotions. On more than one occasion I made sure my family knew I was happy, unafraid, and loving the work I was doing. As one paragraph explodes with the zeal of absorbing unfamiliar sights and sounds, the next describes a total shutting down of feelings that were unable to surface and therefore described as being "numb".

NOTE: Current reflections or commentaries have been added following some letters and are shown in italics.

August 3, 1969 (from San Francisco International Airport before leaving for Vietnam).

You wouldn't believe the room I'm in!! It's much fancier than in the picture, in fact the nicest I've ever seen. I even rode to my room from the main lobby in what looks like a golf cart. Ha! I had a real good meal on the plane and pretty scenery. I'm going to rest a few minutes and then stroll around. More tomorrow. Love, from me.

While staying at the Hotel in San Francisco before flying to Vietnam I recall watching a television broadcast of the first manned space landing on the moon. As I watched the surreal pictures of men actually walking on the moon, I began to feel like I too, was headed for an otherworldly experience.

Later, in Vietnam, I would hear GI's describe returning home as going, " back to the world".

August 14-15, 1969 (In flight between Hawaii and Wake Island in route to Vietnam).

On Wake Island we will stop for 30 minutes to refuel. When we left Hawaii it was 4:30 p.m. & 7:30 p.m. in San Francisco. It keeps getting earlier in the day and I keep getting sleepier...Ha!

Where to begin? I met the nicest Pan Am ticket agent in Frisco. He gave me a fabulous book telling facts about major cities around the world, made my hotel reservation in Tokyo, got me a seat with the best view of Diamond Head, and when he got off duty he met me in time to talk a few minutes and get this—he carried my tote bag all the way on the plane to my seat!!! Honest! Now get this – I sat next to a lovely couple and he joked all the way. Near the end of their trip (in Hawaii) I asked what he did in Dallas; well he is head Methodist minister at Lover's Lane Church and has spoken all around the world. I really forgot his name but its like Dr. Tom?? The family in front of me, are missionaries going to Indonesia.

We had a fabulous lunch of white wine, hard roll cheese, baked chicken and rice, shrimp salad, and whipped cream custard topped with apricot sauce. It was really delicious. We were also given java juice, Hawaii Suntan Lotion, and a steaming hot towel to wipe our hands on. I can just see you all grinning about now…

My newest acquaintance is a girl from Korea who is also spending the night in Tokyo. Right now she has me stocked with 3 pillows and a blanket. Not too spoiled huh? More later, we're being fed again…

Later – Oh well; same ole stuff – shrimp cocktail, cheese from Finland, green salad with artichoke, string beans with almonds, braised beef bourgeoisie, blueberry pudding and tea. Sigh!!!!

My only regret is that you all can't be here with me but you are so much here in spirit that I can just hear Mom "ooing" and "awing" over the food.

Well, it should be about 10:00 pm San Francisco time so I will try to get some sleep even though outside my window the sun is brightly glowing on the putty clouds.

I love you, Bette (God's very spoiled child)!

It occurs to me that nowadays it is interesting that Pan Am Airlines is not even in business anymore. Secondly, having a ticket agent go to all that trouble and give that much personal attention is probably unheard of.

Written on a post card:
When we landed on Wake Island it really smelled salty and fishy and was quite warm but was really kind of cute and quaint and I would like to have seen more. It looked like it was strictly military. It was here that we finally saw the sun set after I don't know how many hours of daylight. We just stayed ½ hour to refuel and it was an unscheduled stop. They said due to the construction of part of the runway in Hawaii they couldn't fill the fuel to capacity. I'm glad it worked out that way because it was just one more place to see…

August 16, 1969
I am now on a commercial plane to Paris somewhere between Tokyo and Manila. After just finishing a refreshing glass of juice I'm feeling great and surprisingly refreshed after getting a little tired last night. I don't know

what this dress is made of, but there isn't one wrinkle even after sleeping on the plane so I've continued to wear it the whole trip.

Waiting for this plane I started talking to a lady who is also going to Saigon and guess where she's from? Bartlesville, Oklahoma. We both had a chuckle over that. She is meeting her husband who heads an English language school in Saigon and she will be there about a month. She said they have quite a few Peace Corps Volunteers teaching there.

I will try to describe the hotel room where I stayed in Tokyo last night. The Japanese style sliding windows opened up to a beautiful view of a harbor, and I was on the 6th and top floor except for the restaurant above.

On my bed lay a starched kimono and slippers under the desk. I slept in the kimono that certainly added to the warm and friendly oriental atmosphere. There was a radio and pay TV also in the room. I listened to a Japanese station on the radio. Pan American Airlines pays for the hotel bill and two meals when it's necessary to layover so I didn't even have to pay that. I did get 50 cents changed to yen to buy stamps for the post cards. A post card stamp is 45 yen and for a letter 90.

Going through customs and immigration is pretty easy because you just get in line and tag along. If it weren't so efficiently run though, the Tokyo airport could be catastrophic due to its size and all the people. Entire families of 10-15 were there seeing people off and greeting them.

I see the stewardess coming down the aisle with something. This goes on about every half hour. They even give us newspapers in whatever language is required. Well, that's about all for now.

P.S.... Just ate and the menu was so pretty. I'll send it to you later. All the time I thought I was eating heart and it turned out to be heart of lettuce and veal. Ha!

Hope you are enjoying the trip. Love, Bette

Written on a post card:
The view landing here in Manila was about the most beautiful I've ever seen anywhere. The hills are all shades of green and although I didn't see these exact rice terraces it was gorgeous. We even saw rice workers and water buffalo.

Sunday August 17, 1969
WELL, I MADE IT!!
My trip was completed without a hitch and my luggage and I arrived in Vietnam at about 5:00 p.m. yesterday.

Would you believe I spent my first night here sharing an apartment with a man!! Ha! Actually, the USO rents an apartment on the top floor across the street from the USO Club. There are three bedrooms, two baths, a living room and a patio porch with a great view of the street below, which is right in the middle of downtown Saigon.

I was met by, Frazier Browning, who works in the Executive Office. He's the person also staying in the apartment. He and a secretary took me to dinner last night, and we went to church and lunch together today.

If I hadn't seen Mexico last summer I would really be having cultural shock. The biggest adjustment is getting use to all the traffic. There are as many motor scooters, Honda type, as there are cars, and they are all over the street and take the right of way, if there is such a thing. There are people and kids everywhere. I had heard that the Vietnamese women are beautiful and that is no exaggeration. They are so feminine even on the motor scooters. I'm crazy about their dress that goes over pants with slits up each side. I'm going to get measured and have one made at the USO this week if I can.

Well, I already know where I'm going. Mr. Anderson, the Director, told me yesterday that there is a shortage of personnel and I'm leaving at the end of next week for Qui Nhon. It's right on the coast (hot dog!) and I will live on the base (army). There are two girls there now and the club is open 18 hrs a day so they really need help. The director is Martha, who received training before me under Lucy Goff, at the Rantoul, Illinois USO. Her time is up in September. I will fly to an Air Base to the north and take a bus on to Qui Nhon through what use to be insecure villages but they are safe now.

At times it's hard to realize there is a war going on here but I could hear mortar fire in the distance last night and from the terrace of the USO apartment we could see about a dozen flares go off to the south. The weather was hot when I landed but it rained about half the night so I was very comfortable with the windows open and the overhead fan on low. I ate American food (fried chicken) last night, but had Italian spaghetti Vietnamese style today and it was quite good. I'm still taking pills for malaria we were given and so far, so good...

Ann, the director at Na Trang, came in today and will spend the night here. I'm glad I'll get a chance to visit with her. I met one other girl briefly at a base about 20 miles from here. She was given a jeep and she painted it bright pink. She has the nerve to actually drive it in Saigon.

My reaction to all of this right now is kind of disbelief. It's certainly another world and I feel so privileged to have the opportunity to take part in it. In other words, I'm glad to be here.

I'll be eligible for R & R during the 4th, 7th, 10th, & 16th months I'm here. It's a maximum of 8 days including travel time in Vietnam that it takes to leave the country. During the last couple R&R's you can go to Hawaii and Australia.

I can't really describe the USO Club here in Saigon because I haven't been through but twice. There was a stage show going on today and about all I could see were fatigues and combat boots as I tried to make my way upstairs.

As you have noticed we do have to buy stamps. At the airport Frazier gave me a $25 advance. Fifteen of that was in military payment certificates (MPC's), which is currency the military must use, and the rest was in "Vietnamese dong".

Well, that's all I can think of for now. I have the day off so I'm just relaxing this afternoon. I'll be in Saigon only as long as it takes to get the necessary visas and papers ready for me to leave for my assignment. More later- Love you all lots, Bette

Sunday August 17, 1969 (continued)

I didn't expect to be writing again so soon, but I want to jot this down before the mood is lost. Ann from Na Trang and I went to a quaint French restaurant for dinner and while there the electricity went out so we finished by candlelight (as a necessity). We had fresh baked tuna and a delicious mixed salad and peas.

We are now at the apartment, and I'm writing this by candlelight. The sounds you hear are the buzz of the tiny Renault taxicabs and the splash of rain on the terrace. The cabs here are a story in themselves. I've seen four so far, in the middle of the street on our corner, that were stalled and being pushed or repaired.

I awoke last night at midnight to a pounding sound, and out of curiosity looked to see – yes, another cab on the rocks…

I understand the electricity goes out quite often due to overloading and this whole part of town is in darkness. Honestly, two days here and I feel that the trip is already worthwhile.

I got measured for my Vietnamese dress (ao-dai) today and how much fun! The little seamstress came up about to my shoulder. She has a small concession right in the USO Club. I picked a beautiful pattern of material that is a blend of silk and something else, but it really caught my eye and I didn't even spend hours in choosing. It's pink background with large branches of cherry blossoms on it. The pants underneath will be white. The cost is $15.00 including the material and labor. I'm sure just having it will be worth that much even if it's never worn.

I can hardly wait to see it. I'm to pick it up on Wednesday. My light is beginning to flicker now so I must say bye for now.

August 18, 1969

Yesterday, I mainly stayed at the club and observed.

I also spent a lot of time reading "Customs and Cultures of Vietnam" by Ann Coddell Crawford. She is an Army officer's wife and was stationed here 2 years. The book is fabulous and quite accurate so I recommend that you read it if at all possible. I bought it at the USO.

Last night I helped Mary Beth at the Zion Club change apartments after a meeting of the Drama Club. She's the one with the pink jeep and white part-poodle dog.

Now, about today. I decided to go on the Saigon Camera Bus Tour leaving from the USO every day at 9:00 a.m. It's one of the most worthwhile and interesting things I've ever done.

There were only five of us on the tour, two Air Force nurses, and two Airmen. Here is a brief rundown on what we saw. Unfortunately I didn't have a camera. Along the street we passed bye, police headquarters, the Saigon River and docks, the food and animal market, headquarters of Korean Armed Forces, the Victoria Hotel where in 1956 many Americans were killed, an Air Force Training School blown up 2 weeks ago killing 16 and wounding about 60, a Shrine for the Buddhist Monk who burned himself in protest to the Diem regime, the British and American Embassies, Independence Palace which is residence for the President of South Vietnam, and John Kennedy Square.

These were seen among thousands of people and unbelievable traffic and sights. The poverty is just appalling, as well as the smells, but all is fascinating.

Now to mention the 4 stops we made:

1. A Chinese Buddhist temple. Hanging from the ceiling were scores of winding coils of burning incense. Each large coil of incense is in memory of family ancestors and burns for 4 months. They are about 3 1/2 to 4 feet high.

2. The Vietnamese Buddhist temple which was larger and we had to take our shoes off to enter. The Buddha was monstrous in size and they were in the process of doing touch up work on that will include a layer of pure gold.

3. The Shrine and Temple of an Army Marshal, Le Van Duyet, and his tomb. This place is fantastic. There were shrines all over and people

kneeling to them. They take a can filled with long sticks, which contain a number. They shake the can and throw out only one stick. They then throw 2 blocks to see which way they land (good – meaning the throwing of the sticks was correct, or bad – which means, throw again.) If the throw is good they go to the message room where there is a poem or fortune for every number. They can interpret the poem in part, but for full details they take it to one of many fortunetellers who are sitting around the grounds making a living in this manner.

4. The Saigon Zoo and Museum – fine collections of Jade. Most were white, and we were told, as it is worn next to human skin it turns green...

Another point I found interesting about customs is that all the Vietnamese staff at the Club are searched before they leave. The new Assistant Director told me about seeing terrible bruises and red streaks around their throats and found out that their doctors pinch them very hard around the throat and upper chest to relieve them of colds, headaches, and numerous other ailments. Our two little guides today both had such marks, so this must be a very popular practice.

Well, I guess I've told about all that I can halfway describe on paper. I came to the apartment following the tour, so I'll go to the Club now and finish reading my new book. Reading it yesterday was a perfect introduction to the tour as it describes many of the places we saw.

You just can't begin to imagine how blessed we are until you see poverty like this. I saw little children at the temples with sores all over them and bloated little tummies, as well as old women who were very sick and probably dying. Until later – Much, much love, Bette

While on the tour of the Buddhist Temple, I observed a woman at prayer in front of the Buddha and realized that although her customs and beliefs differed from mine, we shared the same sincere devotion to a Higher Power of our own understanding. This had a profound affect on my worldview and spiritual life that I am grateful for to this day.

August 19,1969
Hi All: After yesterday's letter I met a nice guy and we went window-shopping and walked about a block to the docks and Saigon River. I found out he was the TV and radio news commentator on top of a hill near Qui Nhon.

Today, I slept late, went to the Club and read most of the morning. Oh, I got my ao-dai today and it fits perfectly. It is very snug at the top and not exactly comfortable but the pants are of a satin material and are just luscious feeling. I'm very pleased also with the material. I'm sending a small piece (enclosed), so don't let it fall out unnoticed.

I found out today I'll be visiting the Zion USO tomorrow and leave for Qui Nhon pronounced "Quin Yon" on Friday.

Last night was the first night I've been bothered with mosquitoes but we've had quite a bit of rain. The electricity went out again this morning... Did I mention the little lizards? They climb around the walls now and then, but they are kind of cute. Love, Bette

Street scene from Saigon USO Penthouse

Friday August 22nd, 1969

Another day gone by and many more experiences. Wednesday night I really lucked into a good deal. Two other USO girls had been invited to dinner by a major beginning his R&R. I happened by at the right time and also got invited. We dined at the top of the Caravelle Hotel, which is a very popular place in Saigon. Most of the news reporters and foreign correspondents stay there.

Man, was it plush! I ordered French onion soup; sardines and cabbage for appetizers, and crab salad. Yesterday, I went to Dion (pronounced "Zion") to visit their USO. Mary Beth drives her pink jeep there every day. It's located in a small village 45 minutes from Saigon. The building is an old French theater and it's really nice. I talked to several fellows who said they thoroughly appreciate the USO being here.

Going through the villages and along that highway were really something. The bridges we crossed were heavily guarded, and we saw many military supply vehicles. Not too far from the road we were on, a rocket went off and I jumped, but its target was far away. Strangely enough I haven't been nervous at all, in fact things are very easy going.

Wednesday, I talked to two guys in their middle twenties who hadn't seen an American girl in four months. It was really an experience just visiting with them, and they continuously expressed how meaningful it was just to sit and talk with a girl from home. Everyone I have spoken with so far is very impressed with the USO and its services. I also got to visit the USO Club at Tan So Nhut Air Base.

Another USO girl has arrived and is staying at the Saigon apartment. Her name is Dale and she trained in Lawton, Oklahoma. She's Jewish, from Baltimore, has long red hair, and is just a riot. I didn't get to leave today as planned, but I'm scheduled now for Sunday at 1:20pm. I feel fortunate that I've been able to see so much in and around Saigon. Last night Sam Anderson, (the big boss) took Dale and I out for dinner. We went to the International House, also very nice, where most of the American businessmen have memberships. After dinner we went downstairs where Dale played the slot machine and I visited with an NCO. I'm getting a little anxious now to get to Qui Nhon. I think I've loafed and "plushed it up" long enough, Ha! Well, take care and I love you, Bette

Saturday August 23, 1969
Hi again!
I've been here one week already! I decided to drop a line this morning because it sounds as though I'm going to be very busy beginning tomorrow.

Last night, Mary McGlasson, who will take Martha's place as Director, came to the Saigon apartment from Qui Nhon to begin her R&R in Tokyo. That means Martha is working up there by herself. Martha's 18 month tour is up Sept. 15th, so after that it will just be Mary and I, and hopefully a third person. I like Mary very much. She's probably in her middle thirties, blond hair, and has a beautiful tan. Qui Nhon sounds great, but very busy. She says we live in a quad with 2 girls to a room and 4 share the bathroom.

Mary says the medical facilities are just fabulous because of the abundance of nurses and doctors, many of whom were drafted for military service. The work as she describes it, is like running several businesses and I'm sure I have much to learn.

I went out to dinner yesterday with another USO staff member, and what a scream! We didn't have enough Piasters (Vietnamese money) to pay the

24

bill Ha! We had traveler's checks, yen, greenbacks, and MPC (military payment certificates), but we were $5 short of P's. I had to leave her there and come to the USO to exchange my money.

I may not have to take the truck convoy from Phu Cat tomorrow because the runway at Qui Nhon is supposed to be fixed and ready for use as of today. Mary says they have been expecting a little action there, but just isolated incidents so far.

The plane I'm going on is a military C130 cargo plane. I will share more about that after tomorrow. We're attending a Hawaiian luau party at the Saigon USO in a couple of hours. All is fine. Take care. Love, Bette

Sunday, August 24, 1969

Well, hi again from Saigon. My flight was cancelled again due to not getting the I.D. cards or some such thing and I think Mr. Anderson prefers that I land directly at Qui Nhon instead of taking the truck convoy.

Anyway, I'm scheduled for Wednesday. This afternoon I'm working at the Saigon USO for someone who scratched her eye with her contact and has a patch, so she couldn't work today.

I've only been on duty for about 1 1/2 hours, but I've been able to visit with the Vietnamese girls working at the desk and I've really enjoyed it. The only real contact I've had with them before is watching them being searched before leaving work. Apparently, stealing may be part of the culture during war, however, Mary was telling us how many things the GI's have stolen from the Club so who can say? Some GI's believe since we get supplies from the government they can be easily replaced.

Yesterday a black GI came up to me with a shocked look on his face because he recognized me from the Guthrie Job Corps Center where I worked as a residential advisor. He used to date one of the Spanish girls and I remembered him especially because he checked on a band for me once. He was sure surprised to see me here in Vietnam.

My dresses have been very appropriate so far. Everyone here is extremely casual and my sandals are all I've worn and no hose even in the nice restaurants. I don't know when I'll have a chance to wear my nice dresses except during the Holidays.

While working the desk today, I talked to a man who had just learned that his daughter, daughter-in-law, and niece, had been killed in a car wreck in the States. I mention this, as one more instance of danger here compared to things that can also suddenly occur to people anywhere at anytime.

Another girl has moved into the apartments until Tuesday. She has been here a year and is on her way home to teach again. She says she enjoyed her tour, but feels it's time to move on.

I've been very impressed with the USO girls I've met so far, and the fellows all speak highly of the USO. You can start sending letters to the return address in Qui Nhon, as I still hope to get there. Ha!

All for now, and love you much, Bette   P.S. It's almost 6:00 p.m. here and you're probably not even up yet as it would be about 7:00 a.m. there... Good Morning!!!

Monday, August 25, 1969

I read in today's paper, the Stars and Stripes, that a district in Saigon got hit Saturday night so I decided to drop you a few lines. We hear mortar fire almost every night, but it sounds very far away and is like thunder. I don't know what you're getting in the papers, but all is well here where I am located.

At work here at the Saigon Club last night I talked to the sweetest guy named Pat Riley. He's a Seabee and travels around Nam doing construction work. Today I helped a USO staffer go to the Vet with her cat. She's taking it with her to the states tomorrow. Three of the little taxicabs refused us service because of the "mow" (cat). They believe it brings bad luck. You should have seen the look on one guys face ha! He said, "mow! no no" and closed the door as he drove off.

I was just informed that I work again tonight. I bet Martha is anxious for me to get up to Qui Nhon because she's there alone. My love to all, Bette

Qui Nhon South Vietnam, on the coast of the South China Sea, lies between Da Nang to the north and Cam Ranh to the south. During the war it was a major seaport supplying military forces in the Central Highlands and was the capital of Binh Dinh Province, also know as II Corps. In addition to army support units there was a Navy Coastal Surveillance Force as well. It is important to note that there was no rear echelon since all of South Vietnam was subject to being a battlefield.

Thursday, August 28, 1969

I arrived in Qui Nhon yesterday afternoon and had a terrific flight. I even got to sit in the cockpit with the four pilots who were wonderful. The plane was a camouflaged C-130 cargo plane. I marveled at its ability to get off the ground because it felt like flying in the belly of a giant whale. When we flew over Na Trang, I got to stand up and look out the front window and what a magnificent view. Then when we prepared to land, the pilot invited me to stand again so I could see the whole city and coastline. I was thrilled to say the least! The water, a rich blue, the mountains and islands, are all really something.

In peacetime this is a little fishing village. The hills behind the USO are similar to those in Arizona, only larger and greener. I share a room with Martha. The housing is also where nurses, doctors and Red Cross girls live. Last night we visited a friend of Martha. He has paneled the walls to his hooch, made a bar and has it really fixed up nice. This is so plush compared to the guys in the field where most of the fighting takes place. We even saw part of an outdoor movie. I like the USO Club here very much. Martha will be leaving September 15th, and Mary will become the Director. Alice and I will be Associate Directors. I haven't eaten yet today so I'm going to eat in the Snack Bar. The mess hall food is excellent and I plan to eat there whenever possible. All for now… Much love, Bette

The aim of the USO was to create an atmosphere that felt like being "back in the world", home, USA. Weapons were checked in at the Reception Desk where music from the jukebox beat out the latest in popular songs like "Black Magic Woman" and "I've Gotta Get Out Of This Place". In the early hours before the USO doors opened, a long line would form for those wishing to get on the waiting list to make a call home on the stateside phone. The highlight for many, however, was a visit to the Snack Bar.

Our USO Club had a stateside phone four days a week; a snack bar with hamburgers, french-fries, eggs and ham, omelets, cheese dogs, vanilla, strawberry, and chocolate milk shakes, strawberry and caramel sundaes, and even steaks. We had one of the largest menus of any of the Vietnam USO Clubs.

We also provided a shower and shave service, ping-pong and pool, table games, and an air-conditioned TV and Reading Room with three beds. Our reception desk sold USO lighters, psychedelic posters, gum, stateside flags and "Flowers by Air". Add to all that several concessions. Three Koreans sold rings and did terrific portraits while the Chinese had a photo and engraving concession.

Some of the troops came directly from the field of battle to Qui Nhon's Red Beach for one day of R&R and medical appointments at the 67th Evacuation Hospital. Grabbing a hamburger and strawberry sundae at the USO Snack Bar were high on their priority list.

Each Friday afternoon, USO staff spent two hours visiting patients and hospital personnel in eight wards, surgery, and the emergency room at

the 67th Evacuation Hospital located on the airfield near the USO. Twelve gallons of ice cream from the Snack Bar went into making delicious strawberry sundaes that we delivered and served.

We three American women hired to supervise the USO Club were especially honored when invited to visit units fighting out in the field.

Transported by helicopter, we took everything needed for a cookout including charcoal, a grill, and eating utensils. If needed, a tarp was brought along to provide some shade.

The menu included steaks, hardboiled eggs, pork & beans, pickles, bread, fruit, and candy. These were a welcomed change from their usual "LERP" and "C" rations.

Mary, Bette & Alice

Qui Nhon USO 1969

Qui Nhon USO 1969

Qui Nhon USO Snack Bar

Bette preparing USO donations to take to the field

GI's checking state books to see if any of their friends are stationed in the area

Saturday, August 30, 1969

I guess you could say I'm really getting broken in. I came to work at 7:30 a.m. and just got off. It's now 6:30pm. I must say that I really enjoyed the day though. I spent a long time typing thank-you letters for books, cigarettes, and other care packages that people send for the troops. By the way Aunt Bid, if any of the neighbors want to send cookies they will be greatly appreciated. We get in about 40 men straight from the field every morning. They haven't been able to change clothes in weeks, so they rest, clean up, and then go to the beach for the day.

We meet all kinds of interesting men here!!! Many are chopper pilots and some fly gun ships. I met a rodeo cowboy named, Tom, who works at the USO Club at night. He's also a pilot. He invited me to a steak dinner and plane ride today but I had to work. A lot of things have to get done before 7:00 p.m. because the town of Qui Nhon is off limits to most military personnel. Our housing called Quincy Compound, is right in the middle of town. You have to go through a portion of town to get from one part of the base to another. Therefore, after 7:00pm the men cannot leave their own compound. This is where we USO girls really rate because we can come and go at leisure from the airbase to our living quarters unless we are under a red or yellow alert. Alerts are: white – normal; grey – maybe trouble; yellow – expect trouble; red – you're getting it …

Tonight is my first night to just be on my own and relax. It seems the nurses don't live here after all. It's just the Red Cross girls, some officers, and us. I figured this out when all I kept hearing were men's voices. Our bathroom is just screened about a foot at the top and you can hear in all the other bathrooms down the line. Our suite-mate is a lady Major, and I haven't even seen her yet. The middle of the quadrangle has grass, a patio, and two picnic tables. I was just talking to Martha about the rainy season. She says she wore white go-go boots (not real long ones) that zip up the back. She liked them real well. Think you could send me some size 8? Not the kind you wear shoes underneath. I can get an umbrella and light raincoat here. Rainy season begins in a few weeks. Thanks!

We went to another outdoor movie and shortly after there was a yellow alert. That meant we couldn't leave the compound we were on so we couldn't go home till it was over (about 1 ½ hrs.). We got stranded at that lovely hooch I wrote you about so it wasn't bad at all. It turned out to be snipers and we didn't even hear any firing. Love, Bette

USO staff housing quad at Quincy Compound

Sunday, August 31, 1969
I just have to relate this evenings experience while the mood is still with me. Mary came back from her R&R today and about 5:00pm we came home from work. Then she took me to meet her friends at Red Beach. That's where they take the GI's who come in from the field for their one-day R&R. We were sent back home for our bathing suits and her friend,

Art, took us for about an hours sailboat ride. Oh! Was it ever perfect! The weather was comfortable, the water was a beautiful blue, and we were surrounded by lovely mountains. As if that wasn't enough they invited us to an informal outdoor dinner of steak and chicken. Art and I played miniature golf, took a long walk up the beach, and then sat in the warm sand and talked. He is my age, married, and tall with blond hair bleached by the sun. He has, a gorgeous deep tan, bright blue eyes, and has taken the actor, Troy Donahue, and Miss America sailing at the same spot. Ha! It seems that nice men are everywhere and there are bound to be some single ones.

What a thrill to sit on the beach and go sailing in the South China Sea!!! As Mary and I were on our way home, we were stopped by red flashing lights of the Military Police. I just knew we were in trouble and guess what? It was the cute MP who invited me to their party the other day. He's one I hope is single. Wow! This morning I was hitching a ride to work and I left my address book at the MP desk. I called the main MP headquarters and within one half hour they had tracked it down and brought it to me. Oh boy, is this ever the life for a single girl.

I'm so glad that I'll be working with Mary. She has a twenty one year old daughter living in Seattle and we seem to have many common interests. Well, I have to get up at 5:30 am tomorrow for work, so I better hit the bed. I just wish everyone could be as blessed and happy as I am.

I love you all…   God's very, very, spoiled child.

P.S. I spent most of the day taking Polaroid shots of the guys and giving them away. It was really fun.

What would the chances be of uncle Dick getting a few live pumpkins here for Halloween? I thought we could plan some kind of program around cutting out Jack-o-lanterns.

September 2, 1969
It's now 10:00 p.m. and I was getting ready to go to sleep after reading your letter, but I just have to tell you about today. Getting up at 5:30am is a brand new experience as you well know, and by 2:00pm it seems like 6:00pm.

Tom, the cowboy I mentioned earlier, is also a pilot and today he took Mary and I on a chopper ride. Oh wow! Was that ever a thrill? You sit there bouncing around in the open air with the world passing by beneath you, or so it seems. I'll find out the name of the chopper and tell you. It was big enough for four people behind the two pilots and places on each side behind us for a door gunner. (Gunners weren't needed for this trip). We just went to Phu Cat and back, about a thirty-five minute ride flying above a railroad track close enough to skim the treetops. We saw a Vietnamese fisherman in a sanpan and I could almost reach down and shake his hand. We let one G.I. off at Phu Cat and picked up three others. I even got to wear some headgear so I could talk to Tom, and believe it or not listen to music. I have to pinch myself to be sure all of this is really happening. I guess I have adventure in my soul because I'm sure eating up all these new experiences. Just think, I could have sat home all my life and watched such things on TV...I finally feel like I'm taking part in the action and "living life".

I've also made another new friend named Bob. He's only 21 and he writes beautiful folk songs and poetry. I'm going to get him busy helping me with programs because he used to be a disk jockey. It's so fascinating to meet all these people in different and interesting professions. Like tonight, Mary and I ate at the Officer's Club with five colonels. (Some light - some heavy - all old, Ha!) Over here everyone wears the same type of khaki uniform except for the pilots who often wear a sharp looking flight suit.

Mom, you're right about me not having time to get homesick. It's also fun knowing that all of you are enjoying this journey with me through reading my letters. I better catch some sleep now. I'll have Saturday off so I will get to go to the M.P. party. Much love always, Bette

September 7, 1969
Last night I went to the outdoor movie at Quincy Compound where I live. The movie was "Gigi", which I had seen along time ago and enjoyed. I think I was the only girl there and being Saturday night a lot of the guys had been and were drinking. The atmosphere is very informal, as everyone has to even bring his own chair. This was the first time I really felt uncomfortable since I've been here, and it really wasn't too bad. It just wasn't the kind of show that kept the fellow's interest so a few got kind of loud and obnoxious, but it wasn't any different than what Job Corps used to be like. I'm at work right now. From my desk I can look out toward the snack bar. I like the way our office is arranged.

September 10, 1969
You should see me about now. I'm with Mary and seven doctors at the POW emergency room that is located near our living quarters. We are having a yellow alert and it's now 2:20 am. I am waited down with a flight jacket because the air conditioner is on and it's kind of chilly in here. We

34

don't hear much firing except every now and then. The doctors are all so nice.

Today, a male nurse, (who is single, and about my age), took us through POW Ward 7, which is for VC wounded other than for orthopedic reasons. One had been shot in the head and one had stepped on a punji stick. There were even three or four women patients. Another was found with quite a load of artillery on her. We stopped at the bed of each one and were told their story. It was quite fascinating. The doctors take very good care of their patients, and understandably are often conflicted about their role in caring for the "enemy".

Today I made my first tape that will be played on the radio to advertise our programs. I start off: Hi! This is Bette from the Qui Nhon USO. Friday we are having a party for Save the Children's Home. I've been so busy lately that I haven't taken time to write because there have been so many interesting things happening. For example, visiting the Catholic Orphanage. We came upon a room with about 35 babies, sometimes three to a crib, alone in the world, but still smiling. Some of their tiny bodies are so frail and vulnerable. I had to be cold and hard or I couldn't have continued walking through there without tears rolling off my face.

Then, on to a room where three mentally retarded brothers lay in one play pen with flies covering their mouths and eyes. We continued to a single room where an 18 year old retarded girl spends her entire life because she has clubbed feet and can't walk. She has become too heavy for the staff to carry her around. I'm hoping we can let her condition be known and maybe something can be done to improve her situation.

Bette at orphanage with mamasan

Party for orphans at USO

September 11, 1969

The alert ended, I slept late and have today off. Gee, there is so much to tell and I just begin to hit the highlights. Remember, Pat, the Seabee I met in Saigon? This Saturday he flew in to see me. He had been to Da Nang to see his father off. I was working that night so the next morning I took him to Red Beach. We had a real nice time and I'm beginning to get tan. The MP party was fun too. We danced in the dirt to a good live band.

You know Mom, when I got the letter you wrote about the sandals, it made me realize that the picture I draw in my letters doesn't really tell what its like over here. The fact is that my brown sandals have been the most practical things I have. I wear them constantly because we are always walking in dirt and sand.   High heels or any hard shoes feel awful and I never wear hose. At the end of the day my feet are grey from dirt.

September 12, 1969

Well, another day and this time I past up what would be a fascinating experience if I had the guts and stomach for it. I just went with Mary to have a couple of her warts removed. Her physician friends, Hal and Bud, did the surgery. They both work in the POW (Prisoner of War) clinic. It's a long metal building just back a few buildings from where we live. This is where the prisoners receive surgery and are kept for rehabilitation. We could see them behind the fence with their casts on and it looks like they are treated pretty well. Anyway, after Mary's wart was removed they had just received a war casualty. He is a VC gorilla fighter who had been

37

shot through both thighs. The bullet went clear through. Bud asked if we wanted to watch the operation and Mary is there now, but you know I'd never make it. He even said it would be pretty bloody. It seems so strange to look at the prisoners and think, THAT is the "enemy"...

I learned to drive the Scout today. It has a floor stick shift and my past experience helped a lot. The GI who taught me, drove by where he works and showed me through the Radar Room. We sat in this tiny cubicle and watched the planes come in on the radar screen. He is one of three here in his class who can bring in a plane manually from the ground.

The 129ᵗʰ Assault Helicopter Company was located at Lane Field, Headquarters of the South Korean ROK Tiger Infantry Division. Pilots of the AH-1G Cobra Gunships flew combat assault missions, and supplied troops, providing air mobility to the Korean Division in operations against hostile forces.

September 15, 1969

I opened up the USO Club by myself this morning for the first time, and so far I've been getting along just fine. You wouldn't believe some of the things that my job calls for and somehow I'm learning to do them. For instance; checking in and out the different shifts of workers, taking inventories, closing out the cash register and counting money, as well as making deposits. Then there are many errands to run and the regular office duties, as well as answering many questions and dealing with various situations that may arise. Like this morning, a GI threw a dart and hit one of the Vietnamese carpenters in the leg. That could have been a rather sticky situation, but the GI apologized. I couldn't determine whether or not he did it on purpose.

Mary and I will take turns working the morning shift (7:00 a.m-3:00 p.m.) and the night shift (3:00 p.m.-12:00 midnight). We are supposed to get a third girl in today, which will be great. Martha left yesterday, so the new person will be my roommate.

Life in the Quad with all the cute doctors is really exciting. We have a ball! In fact, I don't know when I've had as much fun as I'm having now. Yesterday, we had a volleyball game going all afternoon and also the day before. I'm really getting a tan.

Last night Mary and I, and 12 nurses went to a party at Lane Field about 6 ground miles from here. The Cobras, who are 13 gun-fighter pilots, gave the party. They are almost a fraternity and they showed us a real good time even though they lost four of their men day before yesterday. They fly four

38

in a helicopter gunship providing cover for the dust-off choppers who go in for the wounded and are not armed.

Life over here is very informal and I have let my hair down a lot, which you would be glad of, I'm sure. You would have laughed yesterday. Doc G, (29, married, an orthopedic surgeon) and Doc T, (32, family man, very nice) both helped me move the furniture in my room all around. Since I'm the only one in the Quad who doesn't drink, I wound up storing all the booze after the party we gave for Martha. Anyway, they asked for a drink while they were helping me arrange the room, and by the end of the afternoon they were both quite well lit. I even went to a stage show at the Officer's Club with the gang from the Quad. That's where we eat when not working. They had two go-go girls, but their act wasn't as bad as I had anticipated thank goodness... The meals are great, with a wide choice of vegetables and salads. The noon meal is just 55 cents and the evening meal is 70 cents. You can also order from the menu and get a steak, shrimp, or whatever.

A New Zealand hippie type stage performer just came into the office to use the telephone. This place is just full of interesting people, and as I've said before each day is a new and different adventure.

I'm almost out of spray cologne and that's one thing that I don't think the PX has, hint, hint... The guys really notice the cologne. Remember cousin Johnny commenting on hair spray after returning from Nam? It seems that little things do mean a lot. Much love to all, Bette

A close friend and member of our Vietnamese staff

September 18, 1969

Well, today was outstanding!!! Danny, the male nurse and I drove through a mountain pass to the leprosarium. I've heard about it from a lot of people, but it's a place that words and even pictures can't fully describe. It's run by an order of French nuns and many of the U.S. military units have donated money for it. When you drive in you travel down a road lined with palm trees, and then onto a road like something from the movie "Dr. Zhivago". Suddenly there appear beautiful white Christian statues and shrines. The buildings display gorgeous architecture done in colorful tiles and lined with unbelievably pretty red flowers. We walked through the church that is all in white with a profusion of green plants and colorful flowers. All of this plus the beach of soft white sand and interesting rock formations. The beach was completely deserted except for a couple of the nuns who went in for a swim and an old Vietnamese fisherman.

When we were out swimming a san pan went by and dropped off a man with a long board. He made his way slowly to shore and it really looked suspicious due to the fact that there are many V.C. in the area. We went up to the blanket to get Danny's handgun and guess what? In a few minutes here came the little man with his board and he was stringing fishing net. Ha!

Doc T is leaving in a week or so and he gave me his poncho liner (that's what everyone uses as a bed spread because it's light weight and is made of green jungle camouflaged material). He also gave me a 6-string guitar from Saigon. Everyone here has been so thoughtful.

Oh! Our new staff member came and her name is Alice. She was working in Monte Vista Colorado as an extension home economist with Spanish Americans. She's very nice which is good since we'll have to live and work together. I really haven't had much time just to sit and talk with her. Last night we all went to the Officer's Club for dinner and stayed for the Stage Show.

Yesterday, I went with a Korean driver in a big Honjin truck to the Valley to pick up soda pop. It's about a 45 minute drive from here and they had just been mortared the night before. That's where Ken is being transferred around the 8th of October. He sure hates to leave because it's rather desolate out there in the Valley and no women… They do have a nice swimming pool though and every Sunday morning a Champaign breakfast with steak and eggs. We've already promised to go see him.

More later, Bette

The road to An Khe where Danny was going to be stationed was a very dangerous road especially at night. I saw many landmarks along the way that were peppered with bullet holes. When we arrived at the place where we picked up the soda, I entered the building with the driver. Soon I heard laughter and realized that six young Vietnamese girls were peeking out and pointing at me. I realized they probably had never seen an American woman before.

Leprosarium

September 21, 1969   9:40 Sunday morning

I was so pleased to get your card yesterday. As I was reading it in the office one of the Vietnamese girls looked over my shoulder and wanted to know what the picture was on the card. I told her it was a bear and she got a big laugh out of it. I guess she had never seen a polar bear...

We were going to a party in the Valley last night by helicopter, but they lost a dust-off the night before so they have cancelled using choppers for social engagements at least until the Monsoon season is over. Mary and Alice got to go anyway with Doc G, and the rest of the gang and they all spent the night. It sure was quiet around the quad last night with them all

41

gone. I couldn't go because I had to open up at 7:00 a.m. this morning.

Night before last there was another show at the Officer's Club. This time it was a Philippine group and they were very good. Afterwards I played ping-pong for about an hour with four of the doctors. It's funny and very nice how close you get to people in such a short time, especially over here.

I went to dinner by myself last night and was joined by a doctor I had seen in the quad, but had never talked to him. It turned out he's a dermatologist. He told me about a cream to help dry out my face. It's been very oily, but I haven't been too broken out lately. By the way its now 11:30 a.m., so that gives you some idea of the interruptions. It's a beautiful day today. The sun was just coming up when I drove to work. For lunch I ordered a hot dog with cheese on it because I was tired of hamburgers and we put it on the menu because some of the GI's saw it and wanted one. We've already sold quite a few this morning.

That's one of the things I like so much about Mary. She is very flexible and open for suggestions. She also feels that we can change days off and working hours if something special comes up that we want to attend. It's quite a change from Job Corps. Actually I enjoy both shifts. The early shift because I have the evening free, and the late shift because there isn't quite as much to do and there are GI's working...

Well, mamasan just brought my cheese dog in so I'll stop for chow about now. Love, Bette

September 25, 1969
To: Number one family
From: Most lucky daughter
Subject: "Greetings from Qui Nhon by the Sea"
Mom, I got your sweet card today, and had to smile about Uncle Dick worrying about not hearing from me for five days. Everything is better than fine as usual. Last night an officer from Bellevue, Washington, took Mary and I to dinner. We went to the MACV Officer's Club and had a delicious steak dinner on an open patio surrounded by palm trees and pretty plants. He's been married before, and is addicted to golf – I'm not interested. It's nice how fussy you can be over here. I really don't mean to sound like a snob, it's just that I'm finally having an opportunity to discover what I like and don't like about the opposite sex. There is always something to be admired in everyone of course, but there are always those little things that matter so much one way or another.

I had a date with Nick, one of the Cobra pilots, this morning. We went to the beach and then had lunch at our Officer's Club. He is a Warrant

Officer. Most of our friends in the Quad where we live are Majors or
Captains. Remember Doc. T, I mentioned before? I took him to the airport
as he left for home the other day. He was such a fine person. He left me
all kinds of goodies like a poncho liner, flash bulbs for my camera, a
flashlight, fan, insect spray, malaria pills, all kinds of things. He is a Major,
but he never pulled rank on anyone. He and Ben are general surgeons.
Doc G is an orthopedic surgeon and is a Captain. Danny is a Captain and
a nurse. We are all the best of friends in spite of ranks. Anyway, Doc. T
wanted to know the address of the New York Office so he can write and
compliment the Qui Nhon USO girls... He's very thoughtful. I've been
invited several times to watch the docs operate, and one of these days I
just might take them up on it.

Guess what my latest adventure is? I cut one radio tape advertising the
orphanage party, and cut another yesterday for the Dating Game. We
drive to the foot of the mountain to the radio station and I just talk into the
little microphone. On the last tape I even had a musical introduction, and
then he played it back for me. It really wasn't too bad even though it sure
doesn't sound like me, to me. Anyway, I'm on the radio now three times a
day for the rest of the week. Then today, when I got to work, Mary said the
officer from the station wanted me to cut tapes to do some of their other
advertising, like for Red Beach, Special Services activities, etc. It's real
exciting to have everyone come up and say they heard you on the radio.
I haven't even heard myself yet, but Alice and I are going to get a radio
right away.

Oh, I almost forgot. We went to an Air Force party the other night.
They had red tablecloths, candlelight, lovely music, and real authentic
Vietnamese food. Their mama-sans spent five hours preparing the food
they had bought at the market. It included delicious appetizers, (the
bottom layer was cheese mixed with wine) and it was stacked with shrimp,
chicken, lettuce and a small bite of tomato, followed by asparagus and
ham soup. The main course included rice paper roll, which is like a thin
tortilla with shrimp, and who knows what else inside; chicken with some
real good sauce, another very strange tasting soup with potatoes, and I
can't even remember, oh yes, fried breaded shrimp. There was also French
bread, wine and Champaign. I've reached the point where I sip the drinks
at least for the toast...

Well, I'm getting ready to check the GI's work and close up for the day.
Thanks for the sweet book Mom.

Much, much love, Bette

September 30, 1969

Dearest Mamoo,

Please forgive me for not writing more often, but I know you have been reading the letters I send home, so they are of course for you too.

As you have probably noticed from reading my letters, I am very happy. I'm so glad that I came and I haven't had time to even think about getting homesick.

The two girls I work with are real nice, and I thoroughly enjoy my job. I feel like the men appreciate our being here and that makes everything worthwhile.

I hope you and Molly are feeling fine and behaving your selves. Who's been winning at cards?

Please take care, and know that I love you very much, Bette

During this time my grandmother (Mamoo) was in her 80's and was working as a caregiver for, Mollie Goerke, in Canton, Oklahoma. Mollie responded to my request for helping the Vietnamese orphans by organizing the Canton churches and community leaders. They met at Mollie's home and Mamoo served coffee to the numerous volunteers. This resulted in their sending many much needed gifts that were distributed by the USO in Qui Nhon.

October 1, 1969

Dust-off helicopters are not allowed to be armed, so Cobra gun ships give them cover, making themselves' a target which allows the wounded to be picked up in the field. Cobra pilots came and picked us up to attend their party and the dust-off pilots flew us home. That was quite an experience and the lights looked just beautiful at night from the open window of the low flying bird.

The two pilots who invited me came in the office the other day when I was out, bought an Oklahoma flag at the reception desk, and hung it above my desk with the message "this is just a small example of Cobra Power". That's just one example of how sweet these guys can be. I was also very honored when Nick gave me the Cobra stick that is their trademark, and one they are extremely proud of. Not many people receive them. Nick, would you believe is thirty, single, never been married, Methodist, tall, and very sweet. He's going to see me on his next day off. I'm sure we can be good friends.

We had a party at the USO the other day for 50 children from Save the Children's Home. They are kids who have been wounded in the villages and their little bodies are so sad. Many do have parents and this is a rehabilitation hospital for them. Some were missing arms, legs, even an eye; and one little boy had lost both arms and still played the games with his artificial arms. About ten GI's helped. One soldier came all the way from another base because he heard my tape on the radio and wanted to be around the kids. He wound up taking care of a cute little boy who had a cast on both legs that went up to his waist.

By the way, please spread the word that these children need all kinds of baby clothes, diapers, anything and everything. They can be sent in care of me and I will distribute them.

Oh, one more experience. I went to Red Beach the other day and Art took me sailing. He also took two GI's who wanted to learn how to sail the "19 footer". We went six miles out and got caught in a little wind and rainstorm, and man was that exciting. I wasn't even scared, but how could I be with 3 good-looking GI's?

I know you're probably thinking that some of these things I'm doing have an element of danger involved, and they do, but I wouldn't trade them for anything.

GI's at USO Orphan's Party

October 2, 1969

I'm working tonight, so I thought I would take a minute to drop you a line. Lets see, what's happened since I last wrote…

Well, one thing is that we now possess a complete jungle fatigue uniform. Mary had to spend the night in a bunker and the rats and mosquitoes were bad. Her civilian clothes and sandals were hardly appropriate. Now whenever we have a yellow alert, even a practice, which we have once a month, we have to close the Club and send everyone to the bunker next door. We have hats, boots, and the whole works. I sent Mamoo one picture taken in front of my Scout that I felt was pretty good, and I think you will really get a kick out of this picture. We laughed and said it looked like back in World War 11. We really do have a good time together.

The other night I almost worked up the nerve to watch an operation. I was having dinner with two of the docs when they got a call that two Viet Cong prisoners had just been brought to the POW Hospital. I went with them and we met Doc G there. Ben took a look at the patient who was an older VC, and said it would be a pretty bloody surgery for me to break in on. That scared me off, so he and I sat in the next room while Doc G was operating. After we talked for awhile I told him I decided I wanted to watch, so we got into the scrub suits face mask and all and went in. The OR is in a Quonset hut so it's not the fanciest in the world and the atmosphere is extremely informal, like a radio playing pop music in the background. Well, as we entered Doc G was just beginning to put the bandages on the leg wound that had received two bullets. It was still pretty messy and the elbow wound was uncovered that had been grazed by a bullet.

We then went to the recovery room where the other VC was lying. He had been captured and I think had been kicked and beaten by the ARVN.

Anyway, he was about the loneliest looking person I've ever seen. He was lying in the middle of a bare room on a four-wheeled table with only a sheet covering him. We looked at his X-rays that disclosed a bullet in the stomach area that he had been carrying around inside him for who knows how long. There was a mark on his back where it had entered. It's amazing to watch these doctors work with their patients, and it's often difficult for some of them who know full well that they are healing someone who could have killed many of our own men.

Doc G and I have become good friends and we can talk for hours on end. He's only 29 years old and a practicing orthopedic surgeon. He gave me a picture of himself performing an operation and a lovely sketch of a bird that his patient had drawn for him. That shows me what close bonds can be formed by people, even under the worst conditions. These doctors were drafted, leaving their families and careers.

Well, it's getting time to close up the shop, so I better get busy. Love, Bette

During their tour of duty, American soldiers referred to the United States as "back in the world" as though that were a place where all wounds would heal and an illusory "home" awaited everyone who returned. That spirit of optimism could be felt in the 67th Evac Hospital corridors among even the most seriously wounded. The big "freedom bird" would soon arrive and Vietnam could then become a distant memory. Although not realistic, those bright hopes got them through to face the next chapter of their lives.

Our medical friends

Picture drawn by a prisoner of war given to his American doctor

October 6, 1969

Suddenly the war has become very real to me. What I knew would eventually happen when I signed up to come over here occurred today. I guess I didn't expect it would come so soon. Nick, the Cobra gunship pilot, and three of his crew, went down in their chopper this morning. They were going after three VC in a clearing and while banking, the chopper failed in some way. Nick has facial and other lacerations, but the worst thing is they had to remove part of his foot.

Some of the Cobras and his roommate came to tell me right after it happened. I went to see him early in the afternoon, but he was sleeping. I did talk to the G.I. who was his door-gunner and he wants me to call his wife tomorrow and tell her I've seen him. He has both legs in a cast.

Another Cobra pilot came by about an hour ago and said Nick wanted to see me. I went right over. He is very sedated and in a lot of pain. He recognized me though before he went under again. The nurse said they'll med-evac him Wednesday the 8th to Japan. The last time I saw him was three days ago in the office. He just had a minute to talk as they were covering the General's chopper. Then he tried to call me two days ago, and yesterday he left a note saying he hoped to see me soon. I can't say I was really surprised because this has to be expected considering the type of missions they are flying. He told me once that he knew his job was important and that's what he wanted to be doing.

Well, Mom, I'm ok. You know, I said the war seems real now, but that's not really true. Right now I'm just numb. I left word with the nurse that I'd be back tomorrow morning.

I'll write again soon. I love you all, Bette

October 9th, 1969

Well, things are a lot brighter now. Nick and Steve were evacuated to Japan yesterday. The day following my last letter, I went to see them and they were wide-awake and looking better. I even helped them eat a few bites of soft food. (Can you imagine this – me playing nurse)? They were in a ward of about 20 GI's and a few Vietnamese. I took them some gum, candy, cigarettes, and bought Nick a lighter. They had a lot of visits from other Cobras. I stayed about an hour and a half and went back yesterday morning before they were flown out. Nick's left leg was broken in about 4 or 5 places and they cut some bone off his right heel but the tendon wasn't too badly damaged. The first day his face was cut, swollen, and he had blood inside his mouth from a cut on his inner lip, but yesterday they were shaved and cleaned up so they looked much better. There spirit was good

49

too considering. Morale is usually high among patients being flown "back to the world."

Right now I'm all cozy in bed enjoying my morning off. It's been raining steadily all night and still going strong. It was pretty cool last night. I wore my boots over to dinner and the rain came up to my ankles. Well, my mamason is ready to make my bed so I better get dressed... more later.

I just had a cold shower and I'm ready to start the day now. We have hot water most of the time but I've only had one in about the last week and a half.

I went to the Valley for supplies again yesterday. Our driver had a wreck two weeks ago and really messed up the truck, so now we have to scrounge a truck and driver every day and take turns escorting them. Our daily door count has been about 1,500 and that's a lot of hungry men.

I still can't get over some of the sights we see in the villages. People go to the bathroom right along the highway. We had to take one of our Vietnamese employees to ride in the back of the truck because men will jump the trucks and take supplies off even when it's moving. This happened 3 times to the GI that I went with yesterday. He jumped down and chased one once but couldn't catch him.

There is a book I'm going to read that the doctor's here talk about all the time. I don't know whether you and I would enjoy it, but they say it's a riot. It's about World War 11 and is called Catch-22 by Joseph Heller. Much love, Bette

October 12, 1969
Right now I'm cozily snuggled in bed listening to the rain. We had to change rooms yesterday and now we live on the other side of the quad in a corner room. The inside of the walls are screened to keep insects out. The outer wallboards have cracks in between and we can see military boots as our neighbors walk by. Got to run. I'm at work. More later. Love, Bette

October 14, 1969
Well, I finally got a minute to relax so I decided to further describe my surroundings. We had the USO carpenters come in and paint the walls of our room (I chose white). The two screened walls will be covered with bamboo so I bought some paintings to hang. Directly behind our room is a road going to the Supply Depot. These huge trucks and tanks go by and wow, what a way to wake up, coupled with tiny shuffles and giggles of the mama-sans about 6:00 a.m. I'm really glad we are fixing our new room up to suit us.

The monsoon season has started and we have had "beacoup" rain day and night. Our cook came to me at work and showed me a bandage on his foot. Their house had flooded about 2 feet deep so he stacked everything on top of a table and beds. While moving his motor scooter he dropped it on his foot. I took him to the emergency room at 67th Evac Hospital and they admitted him because it was becoming infected. Then accompanied by our interpreter I drove to his house to inform his wife. I was told he has two wives who are sisters, and a girlfriend. I met both wives. One has 6 children, the other none. This was the most I had driven through town in the busy traffic and rutted roads and it didn't even bother me. The hills are all becoming so green and pretty with the rains. This afternoon the sun came out and it was like a pretty spring day back home.

Mom, you said I don't seem far away to you and I feel the same way. I heard that Na Trang got hit a couple days ago but it's been real quiet here. I enjoyed the newspaper clippings you sent. We do get papers from big cities at the USO but I just don't take the time to read them.

Ohh---ick!!! They are spraying and it really smells bad. This is done every day for mosquitoes that haven't been too bad actually. The big thing is roaches and you get where you just flick them off… It seems we have a spray for everything.

I got the cologne and freshener and like them very much. The guys really enjoy the nice smells. Our doctors are leaving tomorrow for An Khe and things just won't seem the same. Doc G will stay on for another week or so though.

I had a touch of the flu several days ago but my fever broke in the night and I woke up feeling fine.

Its time to "chop chop" so I'll say "chow" for now. Love, Bette

Most of our field visits were to units of the 4th Battalion, 503rd Infantry, 173rd Airborne Brigade located at LZ English and North English. Their units were spread across the An Do Valley and they were known as the "Sky Soldiers". We knew them mostly as "the Herd" due to the close bonds that were formed on the battlefield.

Visits were held at landing zones where we could be dropped off by helicopter. I was personally never in an area during a gun battle, and never witnessed wounded or deceased GI's outside of the Hospital. This means that I can in no way directly relate to the horrors of those in combat. I've always been sensitive to acts of violence and could never profess to being "hard corps".

October 20, 1969

Thanks so much for the Halloween goodies. Doc G was there and we really got a kick out of opening the box. Everything looked just like a good old-fashioned Halloween. I plan to use the decorations here at the Club. We have an average door count now of about 1,300 so that's a lot of guys that will enjoy them.

Yesterday, we had a very interesting day. Mary, Alice, and I took a chopper up to Bong Son, actually LZ (Landing Zone) English, Headquarters for the 173rd Airborne Brigade. An MP friend of ours escorted us. We took four big mailbags full of cigarettes; cards; mirrors; candy, etc. that folks had sent from home. We visited the MP headquarters, ate at the EM (enlisted men's) mess hall, saw patients in the small field hospital, and talked to men at a work site. The receiving room at the hospital is down under the ground, and is called the pit, which is a very appropriate name. There was one pilot getting a bullet removed from his leg when we got there. It must not have been too bad because he got dressed and I talked with him, saw the bullet, and the hole it left in his pants. As we were getting ready to leave we saw three choppers take off. The men were dressed in full field gear and were going to be dropped off in the boonies to hunt for Charlie (VC) and report his whereabouts.

Our escort turned out to be an "Okie" from Shawnee. He is an MP, and he was so tickled to see a girl from back home. He gave me a ring that was made over here and insisted I keep it. It's 18 carat gold and has a Korean symbol on it. It's a man's ring and I felt funny taking it so if I see him again I'll try to give it back.

I had a terrible headache when I got home, so one of the doctors went to the Club and brought back a sandwich for me. He is leaving tomorrow to join our other friends at the 17th field hospital in An Khe. We sure do miss them.

We heard today that the movie theater got blown up downtown and 6 people were killed. There shouldn't have been any Americans there because the town is off-limits to GI's, but we have driven by there several times. You asked if I drive the Scout very much and Mary just laughed and laughed when she heard that. We have all kinds of errands to do every day that involve taking the car such as: going to get mail; make a deposit at the bank; go to the message center etc. We also pick up various supplies located on different compounds. Each military compound is surrounded by the town of Qui Nhon and is separated only by a wire fence.

I got a letter from Nick today. He wrote it from Japan and he was leaving the next day for Fort Gordon, Georgia. They took off most of his right foot in Japan and he said it will be at least a year before he can walk again. I called the Cobras tonight at Lane field to tell them I had heard from him. They are all so sweet and they come by to see me every time their choppers land. The other day four of them got a truck all the way from Lane Field and they went with me to the Valley to get milk, ice cream, and bread for the USO Snack Bar. It was their day off and that's the way they chose to spend it.

I got a lovely letter from the lady in Canton, Oklahoma who is heading the committee to get clothing for the orphanage. I'll write her as soon as I can find out exactly what is needed the most. Last week we went with a nun to see a Catholic School, but most of all she wanted to show us the pigs that are fed partially by the scraps from our USO kitchen. She was Vietnamese and couldn't speak English, so we had quite a time communicating. I was driving and she took us down roads you just wouldn't believe. One was so narrow that I could just about run over the feet of children sitting in the doorways. Can you imagine living with no running water and no electricity? I saw a girl the other night trying to read by a gas lantern and it made me think about stories I use to read about Abe Lincoln. We saw children dipping water from a well that if we drank from, we would most likely die.

I'm working tonight, but I got to go out to a dinner party across the airfield. We had roast pork and beef, baked potatoes with sour cream (one thing we don't get much of) and even corn on the cob. They were a group of pilots who can get fresh vegetables from the mountain village of Da Lot, which I understand was held by the French and is still a paradise. Well, it's closing time, so I better go. Love to you all, Bette

October 25, 1969
This week has really been great! On Thursday, my day off, Sam flew in from Lane Field. He's one of the Cobra pilots. We went to the beach and had a real nice time. Earlier that morning, Mary and I got up at 7:15 a.m. and flew with a pilot friend down the coast to Song Cau in an Otter, which is a small fixed wing with one propeller in the middle. The landing strip was tiny and after we landed and turned around a pig ran across the airstrip. We walked through the village looking for shrimp, which the place is well known for, and the market place was fascinating. I took quite a few color slides. The fish were just beautiful. Flying along the coast was terrific and it's so much fun to know the pilots. An "Otter" has seats for

about 10 passengers. That same night we were invited to a party across the bay at Market Time Naval Base. Most of the Americans are leaving and turning it over to the Vietnamese. We stayed there until 2:00 a.m. I got home at 3:00 a.m. riding in the back of a ¼ ton truck, and got up at 6:15 a.m. to go to work... Last night we went to a party at Red Beach, and tonight we are invited to the Merchant Seaman's Club. Sunday we will join some civilians who are military investigators whose job is to learn about enemy activities etc. Needless to say I'm having a ball and still meeting all kinds of interesting men.

Got to run to the Post Office now. I go this afternoon to make radio tapes. Love you much, Bette

Trip to Song Cau in an Otter

Thursday October 30th, 1969

Today is my day off and I'm thoroughly enjoying it. I slept till 11:00 a.m. It has been raining off and on so it's real nice to be cozy inside. I wish you could see our room right now. Yesterday, Toby called and asked me to meet him over at Buffs Den. He brought ten gorgeous long stem red roses and a beautiful brightly colored Montagnard blanket. One of the Otter pilots and Mary had flown to Da Lot and Alice and I received these lovely gifts. The flowers certainly look lovely in our room. Some friends are coming over tonight to put in a paneled closet that they built for us. We really appreciate everyone's thoughtfulness.

I flew with Sam to Lane Field yesterday and had steak lunch with he and four other Cobra pilots in their Officer's Club. The food was delicious and I sure enjoyed the morning. I took several picture slides in the chopper and I sure hope they turn out. Sam left his chopper there because he was leaving later for Australia, so we caught a ride back with four guys who were going on a mission and they dropped us off.

Mom, you asked about the meat and food we eat. Everything we get in the mess halls and serve at the USO is sent directly from the states.

I heard myself on the radio for the first time today. It was just advertising our Sadie Hawkins Day Contest next month. I also made one saying "This is AFVN Radio, Qui Nhon". That stands for Armed Forces Vietnam.

I'll be going on R&R sometime next month, but I can't decide where to go. I might go with Dale, the girl I met in Saigon. If we can't work something out, I might go with some of the guys. I just can't see going by myself to some of these places. It will probably be Singapore, Hong Kong, or Bangkok. Who knows??? I love you, Bette

Sunday, November 2, 1969
I have to take time and tell you about my fun weekend. Friday night I was invited to a private party given by the Director of the Merchant Seaman's Club. It's located of course down by the docks and has a beautiful view of the harbor. It was a Halloween costume party and I wore the Vietnamese dress I had made in Saigon. I had lots of compliments. I met a real nice guy there from Seattle who went to Roosevelt, and graduated in "61. I sure enjoyed visiting with him because we had so much in common. I had met his roommate at the previous party and he is from Oklahoma. Imagine!

Yesterday I flew to Phu Cat to a party given by the 389th Tactical Fighter Squadron. They are the Phantom Jet pilots. Every 3 months they have a Christmas Party, so everyone can have Christmas in Nam. I was the only American civilian. Most of the girls were Army and Air Force nurses.

We arrived at the Operations Club Room which was beautifully decorated with Christmas ornaments and were given an hour to change for dinner which was held at the Officer's Club. They really went all out. There were orchids flown in by Phantom Jet from the Philippines. Each corsage was by our plate. For dinner we had both lobster and steak, baked potato, salad, peas, and wine. There was a dance following dinner. We stayed in the officer's rooms that were arranged like a motel. I had a private room and sure slept good.

We met at 10:00 a.m. for breakfast by candlelight. I even got to see the room where all their flight suits and equipment is kept. I don't know how they manage to wear so much gear. I always did love to see jets fly over, and I'll appreciate them even more now. All the pilots wore their new party flight suits that are bright red with neat looking patches on them, some insignias, and others telling how many missions they have flown. The past week their main missions have been to support a Special Forces camp near the Cambodian border.

Well, that's my exciting weekend. What a war zone!!! Believe me, it's not like this for everyone, as you well know. Everyday, we also meet brave grunts from the field with several days beard growth, torn jungle fatigues, and worn out boots. Each man has a job to do, and he does it well. Love, Bette

October 29, 1969

I received the package of perfumes you sent on the 27th, and they sure are pretty. Would you believe just now one of the guys walked in the office and said, "Wow, it sure smells good in here". I just left home after spraying myself with "Unforgettable".

Remember Sam, one of the Cobras? I'm waiting for him to get a chopper from across the field and come pick me up. We are flying out to Lane Field for a while. That's where all the Cobras are stationed. Two pilots were shot down night before last. Dust-off picked them up right away and only one man was shot. He's going home, but it wasn't too serious. You should have seen the four men that were involved tell about it yesterday. When they hear that a Cobra gun-ship goes down, they all go into action.

I got a letter from Nick yesterday, the pilot I mentioned earlier, and it seems he also has a broken neck. In the hospital here, he kept complaining about his neck hurting and the nurse kept saying that he was going to have to get used to being uncomfortable. It will be at least a year before he recovers well enough to try walking, but his spirit still sounds good.

We've made some new friends that I haven't told you much about yet. They are the group of Otter, (fixed wing) pilots. They live and have a Club across the airfield called Buffs Den. We have gone over several times for dinner because one of them is a real good cook. Last night, Toby, took me to dinner at the Officer's Club. I had fried oysters. He stayed near Pleiku in a Special Forces camp for 2 1/2 months, and he was telling me all about the Montagnard tribesmen surrounding the camp. It was so interesting. He told about seeing a woman in a field who started digging a hole in the ground. The fellow with him said to watch closely. She then squatted over the hole, and would you believe had a baby. A few minutes later, one of the men working in the field came by and cut the umbilical cord. The woman stood up, cleaned off the baby, and walked away. Toby said he could hardly believe his eyes. He also saw pictures of a woman who had been attacked by a tiger which had ripped her arm completely off. She had gone around for two weeks like that until some Special Service soldiers went to the village and patched her up. Amazing huh?

Lately I've met several guys who have come into Qui Nhon straight from the field to report to the hospital for various reasons. One darling guy came bombing into the office one day. We talked for a while and he came back later bringing me some perfume. He returned a few days ago on his way to the doctor, and they admitted him to the 67th for medevac to Japan so they can operate on his arm. I went to visit him the other night at the hospital and we spent the evening walking around the grounds located right at the end of the landing strip of the airfield. It was really neat to watch the planes come and go just a stone's throw away. There also happened to be quite a bit of air action on the other side of town so we watched the flares and tracers. He is only 21, and like many of the GI's he smokes pot, but I thoroughly enjoyed visiting with him.

Well, I've just about run out of chatter, so I'll sign off for now. Happy Halloween!

November 8, 1969

For Halloween we used all the decorations you sent and served a chicken, hamburger, and hot dog barbeque outside on the USO patio. My day off, Mary and I got up at 6:00am and had breakfast at the Officer's Club. We were then met at the docks and took a small skimmer across the harbor to the Naval Base called Market Time. It was raining and we got soaking wet, but had lots of fun. We were invited for the Change of Command Ceremony at which time the Coastal Surveillance Corps, was turned over to the Vietnamese Navy. It was really seeing history in the making. There were only a few guests present and we were the only women.

The General who is 2nd in command in Vietnam was there and all the Navy men were dressed in their nice looking white uniforms. I wish I could have taken pictures, but I forgot my flash bulbs... Most of the Americans have left already except for a few advisors.

Dr G called me from Ahn Khe the other night. Those poor guys are being attacked almost every night. Thank goodness the VC haven't hit the hospital. As a matter of fact, there has been more action in the past week and a half than in all of last month. The NVA are thick near Ahn Khe and blew up a bridge and POL dump two nights ago. They almost overran two camps about 6 miles from LZ English where we took those gift boxes.

Steve, one of my Cobra friends, came by today and said his gunship got hit again and they have even been flying night missions in bad weather.

I wish there were some way to describe the sights, sounds, and people here. We get along great with the approximately thirty Vietnamese on staff at the USO and this makes it even more difficult to see the conditions they must live with.

Qui Nhon is unbelievably dirty and poor. The older women chew Betel nut for a feeling of euphoria, so their teeth are either all black or missing, and it turns their lips red. The young girls that we see a lot of are prostitutes lining the street outside the base, wearing tight fitting American type clothes and lots of makeup. During rainy season the rats and mice have moved inside and some nights you can see several. We set traps in the USO Club and killed 3 just last night. There is also one in Mary's room. I just hope he doesn't wander in here. We brought in a little lizard to eat up some of the roaches. Haven't seen him since, but we were told he won't leave. Mosquitoes have awakened me the last two nights. I sprayed everything including myself but it didn't help much. I might get a mosquito net if this keeps up. They aren't bad until about 4:00 a.m. We still don't have any hot water.

I took Nick to the orphanage and he is going to get canned goods for them. I'm sure he will do whatever he can. Several other units are also going to help.

Now for a word of cheer! I'm going on R&R to Bangkok. I'll leave for Saigon on the 17th of November and go to Bangkok the 18th – 23rd. Then is when I plan to do my Holiday shopping, so if you get any packages from there please don't open them until Christmas. I'm going by myself and hope to stay at the President Hotel.

Now about my Christmas list…I've thought about it a lot and Mom really, I have so much and don't want to get a bunch of things and have to worry about getting them home. We can buy just about everything we need at the PX except clothes. I could use some underwear, but I would most enjoy some pictures from home.

The guys are still raving about the perfume. Got to run. Love, Bette

November 14, 1969

Well, the pendulum swings, so here comes a little sadness and a bunch of goodies.

Remember LZ English where we took the sacks of gifts by chopper? The Cobras have been flying up there for a couple of weeks, and three nights ago English really got hit and the NVA even broke the perimeter.

Two GI's were killed and about 25 injured. The M.P. from Poteau, Oklahoma who arranged our trip up there was hit with frags, but he's doing fine. They hit his hand, side, and a little in his neck, but I visited with him today and he should be back on duty in about a week. He was in the door of his hooch going after his gun when he heard the rocket coming, so he dove outside toward the bunker and his hooch was blown up.

There has been a lot of stepped up activity all around. Camp Granite was hit the other night and also the ARVN camp right across from Red Beach. I went down there for dinner tonight and really enjoyed the waves and sand, and stars.

There was a seven-year old Vietnamese girl in the hospital ward today who has been there 7 months. Her parents, brothers, and sisters, were all killed by the V.C. and they left her for dead. She's all messed up but she smiles and gets around pretty well on her crutches. She's good for morale in Ward 4 and the guys are also good for her.

Yesterday, I flew a plane for the first time. We were invited to fly to Da Lot and I got to be co-pilot after we were flying level. That was in a fixed wing Otter. Mary took a picture of me and I hope it turns out. I started my Christmas shopping there and they actually have pine trees since it is a higher elevation. Nine of us went on the trip and had dinner in a French restaurant.

I'm getting sleepy now so better go. Much, much love always, Bette

Bette in Otter co-pilot seat

Sunday November 16, 1969   1:30 a.m.

Tomorrow I leave for Saigon, and then off to Bangkok on Tuesday for my R&R.

Today, I was in charge of a party for 62 children from the Orphanage. We served sandwiches, pop, and ice cream, and the children played several games. About 8 GI's helped and I wish you could have seen their expressions. They are so good and love kids of any kind. I'm enclosing a few pictures taken today.

The 17th Field Hospital was hit in Ahn Khe last night and even a couple of the nurses got frag wounds. Thankfully no one was killed and none of our doctors were injured.

Oh! I got my Christmas tree in the mail yesterday. It's sure a good thing it was marked with my name and yours on the inside because our Vietnamese girls opened it and discarded the wrapping. I bet Uncle Dick thought of that! I better get some sleep now. Love to all, Bette

Tuesday November 19, 1969   (R&R in Bangkok, Thailand)

You think this stationery is fancy, you should see this hotel (Siam Inter-Continental). The only way I can describe it is, Wow! I'll be taking lots of pictures to send you. I stayed all night in Saigon last night at the USO apartment and was so tired I went to bed at 9:00 pm. My plane left at noon today. We landed in Cambodia for ½ hour and arrived in Bangkok about 1½ hours later. I flew Air Viet Nam. Cambodia sure looked fascinating. The houses were on stilts. Two interesting men sitting next to me on the flight were from Belgium.

When I arrived at the Hotel, I took a luxurious bath in "hot" water and went directly to the pool that I can get to by walking out my back door. There seem to be mostly Americans staying here. I have to get ready for dinner now, so more later.

Later – I met an American couple, and a guy named Ron from Edinburgh, Scotland at the pool, and they invited me to dinner. We dined at the President Hotel with service like you wouldn't believe. I wore my black lace dress and silver shoes and bag. We ate Chateaubriand and was it good! Afterwards, Ron and I went to the Hotel Club to dance and mostly talk.

Wednesday November 20, 1969
Expecting to go on a tour with many people, I was greatly surprised to discover I was being met by a staff member of the Thai Gem's Factory. I was introduced to the owner yesterday by a girl I met from Australia who invited me to go on the tour. It just so happened I was the only one signed up, so I had my own personal guide. We were met at the docks by two fellows in a small boat, and while hundreds of other tourists crowded onto their boats, there I was . . .

It was at least a forty-five minute trip by boat down a river with narrow canals, to the market that was merely a variety of san-pan-like boats selling beautiful fruits and vegetables. The canal was lined with houses and this is their means of buying daily food. Some covered boats passed which are homes for families who never leave their boat. They catch rainwater for drinking and bathing, and wash dishes in the canal or river. We passed many temples and a Buddhist Monastery. It seems that many Thai men join a group of monks for a three-month class as novices, and must go begging for food early in the morning just like the monks. They don't pay rent but donate money for their room. During this time they must pray and keep pure thoughts. This occurs before marriage in a young mans life, and is to pay respect and repay his family for their care.

Each house (no matter how rich or poor) has a tiny structure for housing good spirits who live there and in turn protect the property and family. The monks come by to bless it periodically and they even leave food and offerings.

We also toured the "Temple of Dawn", and the place where royal barges are being repaired. They are used only once a year for a procession.

Pan, my guide was very nice (part Chinese and part Thai). He bought me a banana, fried bananas, and rice candy. He also paid for my cab fare to the store. Needless to say, by this time I felt more than slightly indebted since I had seen shoppers the day before buying about 17 rings in one sitting. Honestly though, I found there was absolutely no pressure to buy anything. In fact they were so busy I didn't even speak to the owner so Pan waited on me. I wound up buying a Harem ring with about nine tiny black sapphires for $10.00, a ring for my little finger with a tiger eye stone $10, a pendant $15, and pierced earrings $3 to match. Everyone comes here to buy jewelry so I decided to splurge. Most women come to buy the big stones or princess rings, but I like rings for everyday wear. I'm supposed to call the store Sunday for free transportation to pick them up.

The General's secretary, Naomi Collins, arrived yesterday at a different hotel and we're going to get together this afternoon, so more later . . .

R&R in Bangkok, Thailand

Friday, November 22, 1969

Today, Naomi and I went on a tour to the beach at Pattaya about 90 miles from Bangkok. There were only six of us who went with a guide and a driver. The Thai guide and I hit up quite a conversation, and he is taking Naomi and I to see the Thai Classical Dancers tonight.

Oh! Guess who Naomi and I had a private meeting with yesterday? Would you believe, Governor George Wallace? Don't tell any of my friends or they may never speak to me again, ha! He's staying here at the hotel in the President's Suite. Naomi struck up a conversation with Mr. Kauffman who is traveling with Wallace and he arranged for a "private meeting" in his suite. We visited for about 10 minutes and then took some pictures with Governor Wallace on the patio. I wasn't all that thrilled because politically and morally I disagree with him, but it was fun! (any comments from Uncle Dick?...) Ha!

I was just taking a bath thinking about the day and as usual, about my family at home, when suddenly they played Clair de Lune on the radio. Mom, I could just see you perched up there on your piano bench.

You know, here I am half a world away and you all seem so near. I picture what your reactions would be to the things I'm experiencing. I can see Mom's eyes glow as I walk through the gorgeous gardens here at the Hotel. Bid's eyes twinkle as I wander through the jewelry store, and Uncle Dick's reaction to the monkeys would I'm sure be much like mine. The monkeys live in a large cage in the gardens and they are really beautiful with long white hair and tiny black hands and faces. I sat and watched them play and cavort around for ½ hour the other day.

I must admit, as I write this a few tears swell up in my eyes, but I can't say I'm homesick because you are all here with me in spirit.

Saturday night, November 23, 1969

Last night instead of seeing classical dancing it turned out that the Thai guide who is studying law, took me to a Thai nightclub. They had a very good show and although there were very few American's there, the songs were mostly pop music from the states. The Club was pitch dark and they have to lead you to your table with a flashlight.

Today was "Tommie's Tour" day again and we went to see three of the main temples: the Marble Temple, the Temple of the Gold Buddha, and the Temple of the Reclining Buddha. The Gold Buddha is about 750 years old and they didn't know it was gold until by accident a piece chipped off, and underneath a cement cover – there it was!

I was very fortunate that my last night in Bangkok was a big festival day called "Loy Krathong". Naomi, another girl, and I went to the festivities at the Hotel. The staff prepared a gorgeous buffet on the patio by the pool. Dishes were served that I haven't even seen before. Dinner was followed by a contest for the best decorated floats which were filled with candles and then floated on the pool. The celebration honors the full moon, Buddha's birthday, and praising the gift of water. It was lovely.

Bette at Loy Krathong Festival Bangkok, Thailand

Tuesday November 25, 1969
Home in Vietnam, safe and sound!
I arrived in Saigon yesterday morning and took a C-130 to Qui Nhon, getting back at 10:00pm.

December 4, 1969
Gee, I have so much news to fill you in on. Last weekend, Mary and I went back to LZ English to hand out gift boxes. We saw some of the damage that was done when they got hit.
The weather has been very cold and windy and in that setting I took my first ride in a LOH-58. That's a tiny "light observation chopper" that seats two in front and one in back. I rode in front Friday night when Mary and I went a short distance from English to North English, a smaller field outpost. That ride made me feel like I've at last seen the war torn part of

Vietnam. My view from this helicopter was like riding in a bubble, and we flew very low, right over rice paddies and hamlets that had been burned and destroyed.

Friday night we attended a dinner at North English for the outgoing Lt. Col. of the 4th Brigade, 173rd Airborne, LTC Accousti. We sat at the head of the table next to the Colonel. He left after the Change of Command on Saturday for the Pentagon and his new assignment. Mary's friend, Colonel Paul Lawrence, is taking his place.

We were the first girls to be overnight guests there and it was quite an honor. They even toasted us. Like me, Mary doesn't drink much alcohol and that night it got the better of her, so I was the only girl to see the Change of Command the next day. She had such a hangover that I had to return alone. I flew with several Colonels in a chopper to English, and then rode in the back seat of a LOH all the way to Qui Nhon.

That was the most thrilling ride I've had yet. It was terribly windy and cold, and we flew so low I could almost pick rice… We soared around mountains; skimmed treetops; and peeped in on tiny villages. I even saw one group of GI's huddled together in the field, and convoys on the highway. Alice and I are going back up tomorrow, Friday, December 5th, to deliver more Christmas gifts. Last time we trudged around in a jeep and went through beaucoup mud.

Today, I was invited to have lunch with the disk jockeys at the radio station. I cut a few more tapes and even plugged their shows. Tonight we put up Christmas decorations in the USO Club and then I came home and put up my little tree. The decorations you sent are lovely, and it looks so pretty. I adore old fashion red and green, and the partridge is so sweet.

Well, I have a big day tomorrow so I better get some shut-eye. Much love as always, Bette. P.S. I'll be sending your Christmas box soon and hope it reaches you. Please send me cousin Dick's address right away. I bought a little something for him and Vicki too…

Dinner at North English for LTC Accousti

North English Change of Command-outgoing
LTC Accousti and incoming LTC Lawrence

LOH-58 Light Observation Helicopter

December 10, 1969 11:30 p.m.

I just couldn't pass up this opportunity to write because it is a very similar situation to one cousin John described about the weather when he was stationed in Da Nang. I am now huddled in bed under a sheet; 2 poncho liners; 2 blankets, and one poncho. It's been raining most of the day and has even been windy and quite cool. I'm warm and snuggly now though, and can enjoy the crisp air that filters through the screen and bamboo. I just returned from a lobster dinner at the Camp Granite Officer's Club.

For Sadie Hawkin's Day, the USO had a drawing for 7 dates with American Girls. Five Red Cross girls participated and Alice and I took our dates out tonight. They were enlisted men and really seemed to have a good time.

Mary is on R&R in Hawaii this week. I've been working days and have been real busy, but have enjoyed it.

We have a great Vietnamese interpreter who also works in the office and that is a big help.

Ha! I have to laugh because as I write this, I can clearly hear the guy in the room across the way snoring. I've never even seen him but I hear him every night.

Wow, our troops just started firing into the mountain! They know there are about 20-30 VC hidden in caves up there but can't find them. Night before last, during a practice alert, our guys were shooting harassment fire and actually hit someone because there was a secondary explosion. The same night five men were wounded at our tank farm.

About 3 weeks ago the Viet Cong shot rockets into Camp Granite and burned a barracks to the ground but no one was killed. The other night though, two soldiers were killed on the airfield at a sharp curve when their truck overturned. I was told they had just left the USO.

I heard more very sad news this week when another Cobra gunship went down. It hasn't been found yet and they think the crew was captured. I knew one pilot pretty well. He came in to see me several times and we had eaten lunch together. Sam said that he was in the lead ship and his buddy was behind him in bad weather. The gun ship just vanished in the fog and hasn't been seen since. Sam has been out for hours searching.

I've received four boxes from Oklahoma for the orphanage and will deliver them soon. We are making a trip to another LZ in the field this Saturday.

Tell ole cousin John I sure would like to hear from him sometime. I still don't know if he's speaking to me after my decision to come to Vietnam. I certainly understand because I know how glad he was when his tour was up in Da Nang. Well, Gomer, it's the best decision I've ever made, or close to it.

My little Christmas tree looks so pretty. Well, that's all for now. Love you all much, Bette

December 15, 1969

I just have to take a few minutes out from under a pile of work to tell you what a meaningful holiday season this is for me. Every day we receive box after box of packages and letters from folks back home. People from all over the country have gone to a great deal of work compiling all sorts of gifts. We get everything from razor blades to a Christmas tree, and even a box of real holly from Washington State.

Each weekend we are flying by chopper out to units in the field to deliver these mailbags full of goodies. This Saturday, Alice and I were accompanied by two army photographers to LZ Pony, an artillery base way out in the boonies. Their unit has been isolated due to muddy roads so even their water has to be flown in. From there we went down the road by jeep to visit with 30 men who are guarding a bridge. They are really hard-core soldiers from the 173rd Airborne. We even got to ride on a big hunk of artillery.

We left a beautiful little Christmas tree in their EM Mess Hall that was donated by Sears Department Store in Seattle. We also sat and listened to the guys read some of the letters that people had sent giving support and encouragement. The silence and attentiveness plus the expressions on their faces were enough to bring tears to even Scrooge's eyes. Some of the boxes we got today say, "We love you Joe, and America does care".

Mom, I just have to tell you. Don't ever worry about me over here. I've never been happier, and this is mostly due to the fact that I feel needed and appreciated. I think when you come right down to it that's all any of us really want out of life. Not that I didn't feel appreciated at home, it's just that my mission is here now.

I was surprised yesterday when a doctor from across the airfield who is a flight surgeon, came by and told me that my Christian witness was not going unnoticed. That seemed strange because I've only gone to church once since I've been here. Then a friend of mine was made Battalion Commander and I took him to see the orphanage one day. He became very interested, and now he has milk and juice delivered every day, plus all rations that before had been going to waste in his mess hall. Our friend, Dr. Butcher, is now making weekly visits to see the children. Transportation is also being provided for EM to go on a regular schedule. How's that for a Christmas present...Love, Bette

Christmas in the field

Christmas kitty in the pocket

Visit to units in the field

December 27, 1969

I've spent most of my time at work during the holidays, but that's the way I want it. You'll be glad to know that during my spare time I have been in the company of a special young man. I met Vince the night before Thanksgiving on my way upstairs at the USO to call home. As a matter of fact that's why I didn't get to call that night. He was sitting out front in an MP jeep and we talked for some time. A few days later he came by and helped me decorate the USO for Christmas. Since then he has been coming to the USO every night. He works the night shift and has had only one night off in three months. He is an EM, and works accidents. About every other night he comes in with another wild tale about his nights work. I've met his Sergeant and some of the guys he works with and they all say he's the best man they have. He's on his second tour in Nam and will DEROS in two months.

Recently, I also met the chaplain at 18th Aviation Battalion. His name is Chaplain Hall from Valiant, Oklahoma. He invited me to go with him to Lane Field this morning to hear him preach. I actually hinted that I would like to go and visit my Cobra pilots. By the way, Steve, one of the Cobras that I call to check on, and who comes to see me, went down in his chopper Dec. 26th, but they were so lucky. Their engine failed and minutes after being lifted into the cover ship, their gunship exploded. Steve was only in the hospital one day, and he came by to see me yesterday. He just had a few lacerations and was very sprained, strained, and sore. He and Bill, another Cobra, met me at church at Lane Field today. Along with

Chaplain Hall, the four of us had lunch in the Officer's Club. They still haven't found the other Cobra ship that went down.

I went by "Save the Children's Home" yesterday and had a nice visit with the British girl who is in charge. She is a nurse, and just finished a job in Biafra, Nigeria, before coming to Nam. She lived right out in the bush. All the children at the home are in some way injured by the war. I took them a large mailbag of donations sent by the volunteers from Canton, Oklahoma. Liz is going to have the children write thank you letters.

Things have sure been quiet around here as far as the war is concerned. We had rumors threatening all kinds of action, but nothing has materialized, thank goodness.

This is going to sound greedy right after Christmas, but I have to ask this one big favor. Before long the summer fashions will be coming out, and I wonder if you could start picking up a few things for me. My clothing situation is getting very bad. All during the monsoon season I've had to wear summer dresses with my two sweaters. They are beginning to show lots of wear and tear. I get all kinds of grime on them during work and mama-son can't get the spots out washing them by hand. They have to dry on a barbed wire fence that also takes a toll. Bangkok didn't have western style clothes to choose from except some very loud prints. I could probably get someone to make a few things here, but material isn't the same quality you can get in the states. You know the type of clothes I like, and what would be practical. Casual sport clothes that are wrinkle resistant would be good. I can even get away with wearing culottes. In fact, they are the most practical things I can wear when we ride in choppers.

Sgt. Martin, the Oklahoma MP from LZ English, came by today and brought me some jungle fatigues, the camouflage type. It's amazing how many "Okies" I've met, and of course they all treat me like kinfolk...

Well, I guess this is enough chatter for this session. I got a lovely letter from uncle Jack and Jane, and a nice card from cousin Marilyn. Cousin Johnny, sorry I didn't send you a birthday card, but I was never at the right place when I thought about it. Hoping that all went well over the holidays, and I wish everyone much happiness in the coming year. My love always, Bette

MP friends at USO

January 3, 1970

Mom, I hope you had a Happy Birthday. By now you should have received the wood roses from Hawaii. I thought they would be a "different" kind of gift and perhaps a conversation piece. I forgot to tell you that we each got all kinds of free make-up (Max Factor) from the Jewish section of USO. It included face powder, lipstick, eye makeup, cologne, nail polish, all kinds of goodies. Then the Red Cross girls left us a ditty bag full of this pen, stationery, comb, soap tray, toothbrush holder, shoe polish, washcloth, and all sorts of things I can really use.

Mary and I are still making visits to the hospital intensive care ward. The five patients we've been seeing are getting along much better so I took each one a milkshake today. They really seemed to enjoy it. I still can't stand to hear them in pain, but yesterday I saw a real bad open wound, and I somehow managed to keep my cool. They are all so brave.

Vince still comes to see me every chance he gets which is sometimes at 6:30 a.m., after he gets off work, if I have the morning off. Yesterday, he only slept two hours before he had to go back to work.

The following will give you some idea of the communication challenges we face. I went to the USO to bring food home, and Mary had told the Vietnamese cook to put 10 eggs and some bacon in a sack for me. I went to the kitchen to get them and there were the eggs and bacon all cooking on the grill. We all laughed hysterically over that because we had not meant for them to be cooked. Then I made egg and bacon burgers, put them in a sack, and started home. I had to stop at a corner in town after leaving the airfield, when two young Vietnamese boys began talking to me through the open car window. I just knew what was going to happen, and sure enough in came his hand and out went the bag of food. I turned the corner, pulled over, and yelled at him to bring it back. To my amazement he did, and I'll never know why.

Today, it has rained without stopping and on through the night. Each evening I have off, I go back to the USO to see Vince when he takes a break at 9:00 o'clock. Besides being good looking he is really thoughtful, and does and says little things that mean a lot. Relationships are sure strange. It's hard to understand why we are attracted to some people and not others. Oh well… I love you, Bette

Monday January 4, 1970

I thought I better drop you a line and fill you in on the latest news because you might be reading in the papers about some stepped-up action in this area.

Rumor is that a force of NVA (North Vietnamese Army), are moving into areas not far from here. Yesterday An Khe, Phu Cat, and LZ Uplift got hit. We were under "yellow alert" last night, and probably will be for several days. That meant we closed down the USO Club, and sat in the dark eating sandwiches and caramel sundaes. Ha! We have a new bunker now in back of the USO that the Airfield Commander says is the best on the airfield. They also send a couple of armed Air Police to guard our bunker, so we feel very secure.

This morning they were working on the electricity so we were in the dark, and now I don't have any water to wash my hair and take a shower. Eating by candlelight at the Officer's Club was kind of neat. After visiting guys in the hospital, all these things seem so unimportant.

Did I tell you about pulling taffy and making popcorn balls Christmas Eve? I was the only one scheduled to work so I got some GI's busy cooking. We couldn't find a good recipe and you should have seen the taffy. It turned brown and sugary so we had a taffy fight instead of taffy pull. It was fun though.

I worked New Year's Eve too, so I didn't bother dressing up. We served free steak dinners for an hour, and at midnight I drove two guys over to Camp Granite so they would have a place to sleep. We saw flares being shot off all around. Then I returned to work and took inventory until 1:00 a.m. The day was actually a great way to begin a new year. I did manage to spend a couple hours at a party across the Airfield sampling everything they had to eat including "raw oysters", ugh!

I'm anxious to get a letter from you telling about your Christmas. I think the mail has been delayed because very few personal letters have come through lately. My love always, Bette

Thursday January 8, 1970
We went on our field trip to LZ Pony several weeks ago. One picture was taken at one of the artillery pads within the perimeter of LZ Pony. We handed them the gifts and then sat down and visited while they read the cards from people back home. Another picture shows us in a six-man crew, M42 "Duster", used against aircraft and ground forces. I understand it is quite a weapon. The part we are in swings around in a circle, and he was giving us a ride. Alice and I also went to visit 30 men from the 173rd Airborne who were guarding a bridge. This bridge is outside the LZ Pony perimeter and not far from a village. We got there by jeep. The weather has been so bad that they have had to fly in their supplies. Ammunition was delivered by a "flying crane". We almost got "socked in" by rain and learned later they actually thought about sending us out by way of that very crane. Ha!

I hope you will make a scrapbook of all my experiences in Vietnam. If you look at each picture carefully you can tell a lot about the country.

Driving past a group of guys at the gate yesterday, one yelled out, Oklahoma! I stopped, and he said I had visited his unit and talked to a friend of his who's from Oklahoma. He said, "you will never know how much that meant, and that's all my friend talked about for weeks."

Mary and I are going up to North English this weekend. I'm looking forward to it.

Well, that's all for now. I'm off today and think I'll go visit the orphanage this afternoon. Love ya, Bette

Alice and Bette in a duster anti-aircraft gun

Visiting a unit at LZ Pony bridge

Saturday January 10, 1970

In my last letter I mentioned that Mary and I were going to North English today. Well, I'm afraid we didn't make it...

We went on "Yellow Alert", last night, January 9th, and remained on it all day today. That meant that we couldn't open the USO. This morning, we brought nine mailbags downstairs and put them outside, waiting for our chopper to take us to North English. A pilot came up and asked where we were going. He said we better change our mind and go instead to the hospital because they had been hit very hard last night. About that time the phone rang inside and it was, Chaplain Roy Mathis, the North English chaplain, calling from the 67th evac hospital across from the USO. He helps arrange our visits to the field. He said they had 63 wounded and 5 killed. Remember, this is the location where we were the first girls to stay all night, and had enjoyed the nice dinner. Major Lewis sat at the head of the table next to me that night, and he was one that was killed. The battalion surgeon, Doc Little, was scheduled to leave for home this morning. He was shot in the chest, but will be O.K. Two Lieutenants were killed and it was their first day at North English. They were brand new "in country".

It seems that the officers were having a volleyball game and a mortar landed right in the middle of the court. One also landed where the enlisted men were watching an outdoor movie. Apparently some Vietnamese who work inside the perimeter marked it off quite well, because the VC knew exactly where to hit.

LTC Paul Lawrence, the Co. Commander, was hit in the leg, but not bad. He also called to tell us not to come. After hearing the news, Mary and I went to the hospital and stayed from about 9:00 a.m. to 3:30 p.m. I just couldn't stay for more than a few minutes in the intensive care ward. I did enjoy visiting with fellows in the other wards though, because some of them that we have been visiting in intensive care have been moved and are doing much better.

Don't worry about us going out in the field, because I imagine we will have to wait till things kind of cool off a bit. Believe me, I sure don't write these things to concern you, but I feel that you want to know the truth, as I would. I just don't believe in shielding people from the hurts in life because that's a very important part of living and growing.

I'm fine, and frankly I'm doing some things I really didn't think I could do, and that is good. I love you all dearly, Bette.

January 16, 1970
I was so tickled to get your letter this morning, and even more excited to get the box of goodies this afternoon. I've only had time to peek through the dresses, but they look just perfect, and the colors are so bright and cheerful. The guys will love them. I'll try them on tonight.

It just happens that Vince is going to work the day shift tomorrow so I can dress up for him tomorrow night. He will be going home in February, but we can enjoy each other's company until then.

I was going to dinner at the Seaman's Club tonight, but it's so muddy and I'm dirty, and won't have a chance to clean up, so I guess I'll wait till

tomorrow. Just this morning I looked at my clothes, and honestly couldn't find a single work dress that wasn't soiled. I don't know what gets on them, but it just doesn't come out. Of course I'll be careful with the new ones. Thank you so very much. I bet you and aunt Bid enjoyed the little shopping project, and you really outdid yourselves. Got to run now...
Love you much, Bette

Saturday January 24, 1970
Enclosed in this envelope is a letter from USO stating that my salary will be increased from $7,500 to $7,950 for 1970.

I'm under Alice's hair dryer for a few short minutes and then off to a party for one of the Australian girls. Only two American girls are invited including yours truly. By the way, Alice has been cutting my hair. She does pretty well too. I'm going to our friend, Doc. Butcher, tomorrow and he's going to pierce my ears. Can't wait to wear the pretty earrings Mamoo gave me. I sure am enjoying my new clothes. Several of the guys keep a count down as I wear each new one. They especially like the short tighter fitting ones (of course). One officer commented at dinner. I said, my Mom and aunt bought dresses even shorter than I probably would, and with a big grin on his face he said, "Yes its been noticed"!

Last night Mary gave herself a party for being here one year. It was the first time Vince and I have had an opportunity to be together in a crowd socially. The officers who are real good friends of mine like Doc Butcher and Ray (the Chaplain) were extra nice and tried to make Vince feel comfortable.

Did I mention that several weeks ago I stayed in the trailer of a full Bird Colonel till 3:00 a.m.? I walked into the Club one night, and he introduced me to Miss Black America. As I left, he came outside and insisted on escorting me to my door only he way-laid me to his trailer that was conveniently on the way. He fixed me hot tea, he drank some too, and we talked until 3:00 a.m. He was stationed at the Pentagon during the Washington riots and had some fascinating stories to tell.

You asked in a letter about going on alert and bunkers. We usually stay on yellow alert for only a few hours, but there was that one exception when we stayed on it for the entire day. Still we can come and go at will. I haven't even been in a bunker yet. When at the USO our staff just turn out the lights and stay put, usually with a strawberry sundae. During an alert at home, I still stay put. They say to pull the mattress over you if mortars are in-coming.

Well, I better get some shut-eye. I'm still very, very, happy and the weather has been gorgeous for three days, Mom, just like you wished for me. Love you Bette

February 4, 1970
It was sure good to hear your voices the other day even if you were half asleep. As I hope you could tell from my voice I'm very happy and everything is great. So good in fact, I've gained 5 lbs in just the last few weeks. Everyone teases me about how much I eat!

Mary & I are planning to leave for Bangkok by cargo plane tomorrow if all goes well. Our Vietnamese staff are off the 6, 7, & 8th for "Tet New Year" celebrations, so we'll have to close the USO.

Vince and I are still seeing each other a lot, but I doubt that we will stay in touch after he goes back to the states. My feeling is that we would discover we don't have much in common.

I'm working on a tan, right now in fact, and spent my last day off at the beach. Areas near Qui Nhon have been seeing a lot of action, but it's been pretty quiet here. Two nights ago though, we saw Cobra Gunships at work and could see the tracers flying.

Sgt. Martin called me from LZ English last night and had to end our conversation due to incoming rounds. Their runway was blown up yesterday, and several days ago, the air terminal at Phu Cat was attacked. All the men are now required to have steel pots, flak jackets, and weapons at all times. That's about all the news for now. I love you, Bette

P.S. Our USO interpreter met me downtown, and I bought two beautiful green plants. People grow them in their homes in preparation for the Tet Holiday, so they can sell them at the market.

February 5, 1970
Mary and I started on our trip to Bangkok in a cargo plane, but got bumped off in Cam Ranh Bay because they loaded dangerous cargo. Rather than going back to Qui Nhon we decided to head for Saigon. When we landed it was getting late so we went to the "out of country" terminal to make a reservation for the next day. The terminal was practically deserted except for a group of stewardesses, and flight crew of World Airways. All of a sudden someone yelled, "Bette, is that you?" Amazingly, it was my good friend, La Rena Brooks, from college, looking just like the last time I saw her years ago.

Due to the Holiday, no taxis were available, so Mary and I were invited to ride into downtown Saigon with Rena's flight crew who were staying at the Caravelle Hotel. We visited with Rena for several hours and then walked around the corner to the USO apartment.

I met Rena early the next morning for breakfast at the top of the hotel, and afterward we went up to the sun deck that overlooks all of Saigon. Imagine running into each other like that, and she was just on a one night stop-over from Australia to Japan. She says she's getting tired of flying since she met a C-130 pilot who asked her to marry him.

Vince came by this morning and we went to the beach. Then I went over to Doc Butcher's and they fixed some soup and black-eyed peas. I started watching the movie they were showing, but got bored and came home to clean up my room. It's so funny, but life itself is so exciting now that movies really seem dull.

We heard there was going to be some heavy action here last night, but all was quiet.

Bette and college friend La Rena Brooks in Saigon

February 16, 1970

Mary is in Australia this week, so Alice and I are holding down the fort. Speaking of forts, I often feel like I'm taking part in an old western movie about the Cavalry. That's because every morning and evening they play revelry and taps. I kind of enjoy it…

Everyone was concerned about Tet due to the widespread attack during this time last year. It's now over and none of the many rumors came to pass, thank heavens; in fact it has been a relatively quiet time. The other night we had word that every large city in the II Corps area was going to get hit, but nothing happened. Mary and I were at a party at 18th Aviation, and our friends wouldn't let us drive home, so they put us up over there for the night in case there really was trouble.

The weather is really pretty now, and I've been sneaking off to the beach every chance I get. I'll be going on my second R&R March 9th. I guess I'll go to Hong Kong. Oh, these big decisions!

Mary said she is going to buy Alice and I a bikini in Australia. All the guys tease me about my modest bathing suit, but yesterday, Vince and I went to the beach, and I was the only girl among several hundred GI's. Believe me, I was sure glad to have every inch of that material!

I'm sending an article about Doc Little at LZ English. He may be in one of the slides. He was playing in the Combo, has blond hair, and would probably be holding a trumpet.

Two slides are missing because right before I was going to send them, a GI came in and said he was one of four guys on a tank at the Change of Command at North English, and I had my picture taken with them. I showed him the slides and asked if he would like to have a copy. He said he sure would. Then I inquired about his three friends in the picture and wondered if they would like a copy. He looked real sad and said that two of them had been killed about two weeks after that when their tank hit a mine on the road, and the third had been evacuated to the U.S.

Hoping all is well, as it is with me. Love you much, Bette

Snoopy tank with a monkey along for the ride

February 18, 1970

Vince left today. He has been a good friend. What more can I say?

My present plans are to take R&R in Hong Kong, March 13th, but I'll be going stand-by and may not get out right then. Sgt. Martin and my friend Pat, the Seabee, might both be there at that time too, which would be great.

Mary and I went to Doc Butcher the other day and got tested for cancer. It's the kind you're supposed to have once a year and we got it done free, so I'm glad. I'm enjoying my pierced ears.

Mary bought me a darling bikini (polka dots, yet), but I haven't gotten up the nerve to wear it. Not much news, just felt like saying hello. I love you, Bette

March 4, 1970

Today has been quite a day! I've been telling Doc Butcher that I wanted to see Providence, the Vietnamese Hospital, because I've heard such awful stories about it. As a result, this afternoon, he and the flight surgeon that works with him, came by for me and we went together. The facility is administered by a Vietnamese staff with advisors from New Zealand. We were told there are usually several hundred more patients than there are beds available, and that certainly was the case. The pediatrics ward was filled with two children in many of the beds. You can't believe the conditions the staff must work under. There are only two places in the hospital with running water.

The recovery room was filled with five or six patients occupying litters on the floor. We saw several with severe burns, and learned that 17 others were brought in a few days ago. They are suffering from a bad fire and most have already died.

Patients are always accompanied by a member of the family who stays to feed and comfort them. That means the family members either share the same bed, or sleep on the floor. Many of the beds were wooden, and just barely hanging together with a thin mattress and often no sheets.

You know, Mom, I just can't get over the strength of the Vietnamese people. I was so stunned by what I saw, that honestly, I was just numb.

After returning to the airfield, we had dinner at the 67th Evac, and I came home just before the rest of the days action began. One of our tank farms was hit, so about 6:00 p.m., while still daylight, our men started shooting rockets into Vung Chua Mountain. The action lasted a couple of hours, and we went on yellow alert. A bunch of us gathered in the middle of the quad and watched the fireworks. Then, Mary phoned, and said Sam tried calling me at work saying he was on the way in his Cobra gunship, and to be sure and watch. I have to admit, that made it even more interesting. The Cobra pilots left several pretty good size fires burning on the mountain. What a war this is…

I'm really tired now after a somewhat unusual day, so I'll sign off.

Much love, Bette

March 10, 1970

Gee, have I had a busy week. Saturday, Mary and I went to North English and stayed over night. We visited 7 platoons of about 25 men each out in the field, and left the mailbags of Christmas gifts we were unable to deliver before. I think the guys enjoyed them more now, even the Christmas cards.

Saturday night we were invited to their dining-in dinner. One Lieutenant is selected to come in from the field, and this week it was Lt. Slaughter, who I had met before several times. He received orders for promotion to 1st Lt, and at the dinner I was asked to help the Colonel pin on his bar.

Those young Lieutenants really have a tough job. They are about cousin

Johnny's age, and have command of about 25 men out in the field. Lt Slaughter's group was stationed on a small hill that overlooked some beautiful scenery. Mary and I also visited a recon team on a beach with beautiful clear blue waves and white sand. One team was in what used to be a Vietnamese school, but it has been mortared, and now looks like something out of a World War II movie in Italy.

Day after tomorrow I fly to Saigon, leaving for Hong Kong the 13th, I hope. I'll be going stand-by on a military flight. Did I tell you that I'll be traveling with Pat? Pat is the Seabee I met when I first came to Nam, and I consider him a friend. He made special arrangements to leave from Saigon so we can try and go on the same flight. I sure am glad because it's so much nicer than traveling alone.

Things have been real quiet here lately as compared to my last letter. Well, I'm really pooped, so think I'll retire. I love ya much, Bette

Creative hooch

War Is Not Healthy for Children and Other Living Things

Visit to a bunker

How young we were back then

Field Visits

Packages from home

A happy moment…

A sad moment…

March 15, 1970

Well, I made it to Hong Kong. I had to purchase a commercial ticket for $130.00 because stand-bys were filled up. The Hotel where I'm staying is only a few months old and my room is $8.00 a night. I have a beautiful view with a park across the street.

You just wouldn't believe Hong Kong at night! The only problem so far is that I am freezing! Mom, I can just hear you, ha! Yes, I forgot to bring my yellow coat that wouldn't have been warm enough anyway, and my two sweaters are stretched all out of shape. The trouble here is trying to find ready-made clothes. The sweaters are mostly all beaded or have lambs wool and shed so today I'm going to hunt for a warm car coat.

A veterinarian friend in Nam gave me the name of a tailor that he and his wife were happy with. I therefore looked up Mr. Chow first thing and he is making me two dresses, a blouse, and a pair of bell-bottom pants. I bought two dresses at the China Fleet Shopping Center and, wow, you should see the sailors! A big ship docked and there are 10,000 in just one fleet.

Pat arrived in Hong Kong the same day and we have been seeing the sights together, which has really been nice. He is staying at a different hotel, but the transportation here is fantastic. The ferry ride to Hong Kong Island is about four cents. We have never had to wait over three or four minutes. Last night we took a ferry to the island, and saw the movie

"Downhill Racer". It was great. It was in English with Chinese symbols at the bottom of the screen.

Currently it is 9:00 a.m. and I'm buried under three blankets in bed and I'm still cold. It's extremely overcast and hazy. I am amazed to see people doing Tai Chi early each morning in the park.

I ordered a beautiful pair of real leather boots for $20.00 and three pair of sandals. This is really something, to have shoes custom made. I sure wish I had the boots for today, but I figure they'll be good in the rainy season back in Vietnam. The food here is fantastic everywhere. I've eaten crab au gratin, roast beef, and grilled chicken. The prices are so ridiculously low for such beautiful surroundings and superb service. All three meals yesterday were under $4.00 U.S. Well, that's it for now. Pat should be coming soon.

Oh, I almost forgot. I bought a real pretty Seiko bracelet watch for $18.50, and a beautiful jade ring of Florentine gold to match for $35.00. Well, you can't leave Hong Kong without buying jade, right?

First thing in the morning I looked out the window at a small park and there were many people doing Tai Chi. What a lovely way to begin the day.

March 18, 1970

I'm now sitting in the lobby of Pat's hotel relaxing after several hours of shopping again and having lunch. We ate at a typical Chinese restaurant and had the following: Duck (Peking style) dipped in a sauce and rolled in, would you believe a tortilla, some fried rice with scrambled eggs, corn and chicken soup, and jasmine tea. By the way, Mr. Chow, who I purchased the clothes from, gave me a whole can of tea and sent one to Mike Martin's wife. Oh, I guess I haven't told you – Mr. Chow took Pat and I to lunch yesterday. We had crab, roasted chicken, and Chinese noodles. I even tasted some Sake, and ooh it's awful. I'm getting pretty good at using chopsticks. Mr. Chow is such a gentleman. He paid for the meal but it seemed like more than just being a good businessman. He took us to a restaurant where locals eat, with no tourists in sight. You just can't imagine the competition the business owners have. Everyday is like Christmas shopping back home.

I'm so pleased with the purchases I've made. My boots are of fine leather, and are just beautiful. My three sandals are also of excellent quality. I had Mr. Chow make two skirts with shorts underneath, and tops and scarves to match. That's for when I ride in helicopters. Today, I found a beautiful store with readymade clothes, and got two sporty looking shirts and a jean type wrap-around skirt.

I'm not sure how much money I've spent, but it's sure been fun, and most of the items are really necessities.

Well, I've got to go now. More Later, Bette

March 19, 1970

Pat left early this morning, so I've had the whole day to myself. I've been glad that I had Pat to bum around with because, as you well know, I never did like to travel by myself. We have had lots of fun together. He even brought me roses and two irises the other morning. I bought a cake for him on his birthday, and I think he enjoyed his leave. That night we dined at the revolving restaurant and the lights of Hong Kong were lovely. Since he's a Seabee he moves around a lot in Nam doing construction work in the field, so he's returning to a not very secure area.

I slept late this morning and during lunch met a fellow from Finland, recently from Australia, who is traveling all over. I also visited with a GI who was on R&R. Then I went to the Hong Kong Hyatt Hotel Beauty Shop. The Chinese beautician gave me a great hairdo. I hope it lasts at least till I get back to Qui Nhon. You know, as much fun as I've had on R&R, I still look forward to returning to work. I guess you can't get much happier than that...I feel so lucky to have such a good job and one that I like so well. My doctor in Oklahoma was sure right, saying that all I needed was to change jobs. I feel great even doing all this traveling.

Well, that pretty well brings you up to date. I guess I'll go take a bath, mainly to get warm, and go out somewhere to dinner. Transportation here is great because you can get a cab and go almost anywhere for $1.00 HK or 16 cents U.S. Love you, Bette

April 1, 1970

Gee it was fun talking to you this morning from the USO. I felt just like I had seen you only last week. Since I got back from Hong Kong I haven't slowed down once. Two days later Mary and I went to Phu Cat to a party and spent the night. I met an F-4 jet pilot who's called twice and came to see me once. When he's not flying he works in Saigon sending jets all over South Vietnam wherever they are needed. Tuesday night Alice and I went to English, and handed out goodies at Fire Base Beaver. We were invited to the dining-in that evening where they gave me a cake and sang Happy Birthday.

Last night, on my actual twenty-eighth birthday, Dr. Butcher invited me out for lobster dinner. When we reached the Officer's Club over at

Camp Granite, nine of our friends were there for cake and birthday dinner including champagne.

A couple hours after we left, zappers broke into Camp Granite, and there was small arms fire. Then, at 1:00 a.m. back at the Quad, I was jarred out of a sound sleep by a mortar hitting. Mary came bounding through the door from her room about the same time. We started getting dressed, and as I was standing at my closet, another mortar hit, and this time rocks began hitting our tin roof. I ran for Mary's room and we pulled her mattress over us as we dove for the floor. About five more hits came while we were there, with more rocks pounding the roof.

After it was quiet we walked outside to watch the flares, and the sky was lit up where the tank farm had been attacked. While fighting that fire two GI's were killed by snipers. We heard today that what we experienced, were seven mortars landing in the motor pool directly behind us. It also appears that every major installation was hit in South Vietnam. Further word so far, is that a barracks was hit at LZ Uplift between here and English, and sixteen were killed, but all kinds of rumors get passed around.

Mary got a letter from her mother last week who lives in Chicago. Her mother said she thought Mary was just as well off here in Nam as back home.

The world situation is so distressing right now Mom, that I don't think you should feel any more concern for me here than anywhere else, and I think you would agree.

Well, I'm really exhausted so I better close. Believe me when I say I've never been happier or more content.

I love you, Bette

April 2, 1970
Received my box today in the mail, and I love the gifts. You always seem to know just what I will enjoy.

And, the swimsuit, "look out beach, here I come...".

I went to the beach today, and was able to go sailing with a missionary family from Saigon.

Got to get home and to bed now. Much love, Bette

April 13, 1970
Remember me telling you about Ken Slaughter? He's the Lieutenant up at North English I pinned for his promotion. He's in the hospital here in

Qui Nhon with malaria. I visit him twice a day. Last night he looked pretty bad with a fever about 104 degrees, but tonight he's doing better.

Alice is on R&R in Tokyo so I've been working fairly long hours. I've decided to go to Taipei for my R&R next month. I'm waiting to go to Australia when it's summer there, and right now its fall and turning cool.

Things have been quiet around Qui Nhon lately. Downright peaceful in fact. I even went to the market twice this week with two of our Vietnamese staff. We bought material so they can have Vietnamese dresses made for each of the women. Mary, Alice, and I will have dresses made for us just for fun and maybe a special occasion.

I'm still amazed when I go into downtown Qui Nhon. It is difficult relating to the sights I see. Everything is so dirty, and elderly men and women are carrying loads twice their size. I saw an old woman who was begging, squat down, (after pulling up her pant leg) to go to the bathroom, and people walked all around her not even noticing because this is a normal occurrence. Of course squatting here is just like standing at home, and people are able to squat flat footed. I've never seen an American who could do it.

You asked about the weather. Well, yesterday was a scorcher, but today was misty and tonight actually cool. Mary got her room air-conditioned, so we will have an escape from the heat, and thankfully our USO office has air conditioning.

Well, that bed looks warm and cozy, so think I'll catch some zzzzz's. Be happy! I love you, Bette

April 16, 1970

I'm off today so thought I would drop you a line. I went to the beach and wore a bikini underneath some shorts, but just couldn't get up my nerve to only wear the bikini. I sat there talking to the lifeguards for some time when one of the Korean soldiers asked if they could take my picture. I said sure, and then we continued talking. He asked why I didn't go in swimming and said the guys were all waiting for me to go in. Well, that didn't give me any more nerve, I'll tell you…Ha!

One of the lifeguards at Red Beach says he was a pitcher for the Atlanta Braves. He said he would be happy to take me sailing.

Last night some of us at the Quad, watched gun ships shoot rockets and mini guns into the mountain. It's 6:30 p.m. now, time for chow, and then I'll go visit Ken in the Hospital. We will probably watch a movie over at the 67th Evac. He's feeling much better from the malaria.

Sunday, April 19, 1970

I'm under the fan (it's faster than the hair dryer), and I just have to share with you the fun events from the weekend.

Cecil, is the USO Director at Tan San Nuit Club, in Saigon, and Liz is from England working with "Save the Children." They joined Mary and I when we went to North English yesterday. We arrived in time to serve food in the EM Mess hall. Most of the GI's were so flabbergasted to see four "round eyes" dishing up their food that they couldn't even look up. We had dinner, and a Korean band put on a show. We learned that, Bravo Company, 4/503rd, 173rd Airborne had been out humping in the mountains for five days, and yesterday four men were hit by a booby-trap.

This morning we had breakfast, went to church, and took 50 steaks out to a Platoon for a cookout. There were three guys there from Oklahoma, so I really enjoyed myself. This location has been having a lot of action at night, so they had been on edge, and really seemed to appreciate our visit and the food. Not necessarily in that order!

Later a chopper plucked us up about 2:00 p.m., and left us off on a beautiful sandy beach, where we met up with Col. Lawrence, the Doc, and several Lieutenants. We didn't have swimsuits so we shed our shoes and dove in. I was luckily wearing my pink shorts dress and it doubled great for a bathing suit. We stopped off at N. English just long enough to pack.

Well, my hair is almost dry, and I want to visit Ken and two other GI's in the hospital. Till later – Love Bette

April 27, 1970

This has been a week of feeling very close to the war. I received a call from a medic at the 67th Evac Hospital asking if I would visit someone in critical condition. As I entered the Intensive Care Ward and approached his bedside I felt such a sense of panic and inadequacy. He had lost both legs and if that wasn't bad enough he had patches over both eyes. He was conscious and naturally nervous. Not being able to connect with him visually and since I didn't know him, I explained who I was and where I was from. I wish I could say that I was some comfort to him just being there, but that is not the way I feel. Sad, afraid, and helpless better describe my feelings.

The next day I was showing Chaplain Roy Mathis from N. English some of my slides and he said that the GI who I was sitting next to on top of a bunker in two pictures became another double amputee, and was best friend of the patient I visited yesterday. Before working up the nerve to return to the Hospital, I learned that both of them had died.

Sunday morning I went to church at the hospital chapel, and visited several wards. Would you believe that in asking questions about one GI who I had promised a picture, I learned that he and his friend, also in the picture, had both been admitted the previous day. The picture was taken about 5 months ago. I visited with both of them and gave each a copy of the picture. They were on a tank and I'm standing in front. One of them is being evacuated to the states and the other will return to the field.

Saturday night I flew to Lane field to a 129th Cobra party. Half way through the party they went on yellow alert and two crews had to go on missions. When I returned to Qui Nhon and tried driving out the gate the guards said I couldn't leave because we were on Yellow Alert, and Camp Granite and Quincy Compound where we live had been hit. About that time, an MP friend of mine drove up and they escorted me home. Nothing was damaged at Quincy, but several were injured when buildings were hit at Granite. Mary is still in Hong Kong so I was by myself, but I went to bed and all was quiet the rest of the night.

Mary will be leaving in July, and Alice will take over as Director. I'm happy remaining Assistant Director. Mary is going to extend and will probably get assigned to another USO Club in Cam Rahn Bay.

I'm sure you realize that a few girls over here take advantage of their position and make money on the side. I'm glad to say none of the girls I know are guilty of that. Just as a point of interest, a round-eye can take in $50 from a GI for one night...so I'm told! One day I had a note left on my car making that type of offer and it startled me because we just aren't treated in that manner. You would be surprised how open people are in discussing such things over here, and it's good because you learn a lot about how different people think. I don't know how I got on to that subject. I just got off work at 11:00 p.m. and I'm drying my hair because I have to open up at 7:00 a.m. tomorrow. I went to the beach this morning before work and got sand in it. It's been over 100 degrees but today it rained hard and then got hot again.

Mom, I've sure enjoyed your letters. Just hearing about your daily happenings keeps me feeling close to things at home.

P.S. Wednesday morning I'm being interviewed on Mac's radio program. I'll tell about USO and our May activities. Tell you later how it goes...
Much love, Bette

May 6, 1970

In this letter, I have several adventures to relate. Lets see, I'll begin with my big radio debut last Wednesday. I was interviewed on the 77 Street

Subway Show from 11:00 a.m. to noon. Mac, the disc jockey, just asked me informal questions about myself, and the USO. In between he would play some records, and I got to make several dedications. One was to all the guys from Oklahoma. I relaxed after the first few minutes and really enjoyed it.

The next adventure, that was somewhat out of the ordinary, began when an old seaman off one of the ships in the harbor came to the office wanting to donate a T.V. to one of the orphanages. I went several places with him only to find that someone had recently given TV's to all the orphanages that have electricity. I happened to think of the Red Cross "Happy Hooch", a new little recreation center behind our quadrangle, so I called them and Claudia, her driver, the old man, and I went to the ship. It appeared that the television had just been given away, but they said there was another one. We began talking to various men and someone suggested we get the captain's approval.

When the captain saw us, he heartily welcomed us into his cabin, began relating all kinds of interesting tales, just like you would imagine, and he invited us (Claudia and I) to stay for lunch aboard ship. Wow! I had delicious clam chowder and salmon, plus a neat dessert.

We were then given a tour of the ship, which was on its way to Taiwan to be scrapped. I found that a shame because it was really nice. They hauled army cargo from San Francisco this time, but their usual trips were to South America, taking about 12 passengers for $18.00 a day including meals.

By the time we got through, we had scrounged not only the TV, but also a Van packed to the brim with rugs, blankets, dishes for the USO, and a whole variety of stuff.

Then yesterday, Bob, the lifeguard at Red Beach, invited me to go with him and two other guys on a catamaran to the Leprosarium. We shoved off at 10:00 a.m. and stayed all day. Gee, it was fun. We had the whole beautiful beach to ourselves. They did some surfing, although the waves weren't very big, and I just played around on the little surfboard. I mentioned Bob to you once before. He pitched for the Atlanta Braves, and there was a recent article about him in the paper. He's happily married and grateful to have this type of military assignment.

I just wish you could visualize what the Leprosarium is like. It is behind some mountains on the coast, in a cove with a white sandy beach. There are hardly any people around and you seldom see any of the patients. The buildings are of beautiful tile, made on site, and the grounds are immaculate. It is administered by a French order of Catholic nuns. One of the Sisters offered us cokes yesterday. She was precious, dressed in her pretty white habit. The area is supposed to be neutral ground in the war since they welcome everyone who needs their care.

After returning to Qui Nhon, John, the D.J. who went with us, invited us over to the Radio Station and we listened to hit records of the past.

This weekend Mary and I are planning on going back to North English.

The F-4 pilot I met last month called and was going to come by, but he got a call from Saigon that he was needed back there. It probably had something to do with the U.S. taking more action in Cambodia. That came as no surprise because we've been over there for months anyway… Remember when I went on R&R to Bangkok and I mentioned landing in Cambodia? There were rows and rows of fighter planes there and in Bangkok as well.

Chaplain Roy Mathis in a lighter moment at USO office

May 19, 1970
Well, we had another big weekend. Mary and I left with Chaplain Roy Mathis for North English at 7:00 am Saturday. I don't know if I've

mentioned Chaplain Mathis or not, but he's really great. He arranges all of our trips up there. He comes down every Friday night to visit his paratroopers in the hospital. He's called the "Sky Parson".

It's very sad because things are quickly changing. Col. Lawrence has his Change of Command next week and will be taking over 5th Special Forces in Na Trang. It's been quite an honor to know him because he's a brilliant man and he has been very kind to the USO girls.

While at North English we flew 30 steaks to a platoon for a cookout, and dropped off a mailbag of goodies to another platoon. We really had a nice time Saturday night. I got to see a captain again who is single, my age, smart, brave and very interesting. He will be leaving Vietnam soon with orders for a promising career.

Mary is leaving next week to take over a USO Club in Cam Ranh Bay Vietnam. I sure hate to see her go. She's extended her tour for another 18 months. With all these changes, my life will change too. Alice will take over as Director and I don't know who will replace Mary as the third staff member.

I'm all packed and I will leave tomorrow for Saigon. I'll fly out, Thursday, the 21st for Taipei on a regular R&R flight.

I have a dinner date waiting when I get to Saigon tomorrow with the F4 pilot.

Guess I better rest up now for my big trip. Love you all very much

May 22, 1970

Greetings from Taipei, Taiwan! I arrived in Saigon Wednesday, and that night went to a dinner party. It was at a Villa downtown decorated with furniture and nick-knacks from all over the Orient. We had a lovely dinner. There were about six couples mostly working with USAID.

This is the first actual R&R flight I've taken. I stayed at Camp Alpha, the R&R Center Wednesday night. This spoiled kid is lucky again because on the same flight are two USO girls working in Da Nang. We get the royal treatment like sitting in the VIP room, a special car to and from the airport etc. so I just latched onto them. This afternoon we went on a tour to Wulai, an aborigine village in the mountains. The scenery was beautiful complete with a waterfall. The most fun thing was riding in a pushcart on a tiny railroad track. Would you believe I even danced with some aborigine girls in their native costume? It poured rain on our way down the mountain but that was fun too. The hill was curvy and very narrow.

Tonight we just returned from dinner at the top of the Ambassador Hotel (delicious Chinese cuisine) and then went to see "Anne of a Thousand

Days" with Richard Burton. It was excellent and you all would enjoy it.

Got to get some shut-eye because we have a big day ahead tomorrow. More later, Bette

May 23, 1970   Evergreen Hostel, Sun Moon Lake, Taiwan

Hello again! What a fantastic day this has been! Millie and I awoke at 7:00 am, had breakfast and set off on our journey. Kay stayed behind in Taipei to shop. It was my idea to take this trip after talking to a G.I. at the R&R Center. We caught the 8:30 a.m. train to Tai Chung, which is a three-hour trip. That was our first pleasant surprise. It was a super-deluxe, air-conditioned express train. The interior décor was red carpet and blue velvet looking, adjustable seats. We were served hot tea and the delightful oriental "cool wash cloth" to refresh yourself. These are handed out on planes, buses, and trains. The train had huge picture windows allowing us a panoramic view of the countryside. Honestly, once again, it was like stepping into the movie "Dr Zhivago". As we rolled along, the low-leveled rice fields began to form hills, and soon became terraced landscapes scattered throughout jade green mountain peaks. I can certainly see why they refer to it as Taiwan's Switzerland.

We got to Tai Chung in time to have lunch at the Railway Hotel. Then at 2:30 p.m., we caught a bus for Sun Moon Lake. That bus rip was something else. The driver didn't slow down for dogs, ducks, water buffalo, or kids, but he did blow his horn every two seconds. The road was tremendously bumpy and the narrow curves going up through the mountains were wide enough for one-way only – except that traffic soaring toward us from the other direction, thought the same thing. Anyway, at one point we had to stop and back up so a truck could make it through our end of a tunnel.

We arrived at the Evergreen Hostel at Sun Moon Lake about 4:30 p.m. Gang – this place is truly unbelievable! All I can do is take lots of pictures and hope they turn out. Our room is on the 7th floor facing the lake and we're high on a hill. We arrived looking quite bedraggled so our first stop was a visit to the beauty shop. My hair was in desperate need of a cutting and the girl in the combination beauty and barbershop couldn't speak a word of English besides "shampoo". Millie cuts hair, so she did most of the cutting and I now have a pixie that's slightly longer on one side, and the short side is cut high above the ear. Anyway, I like "different" and it will be real practical.

We just finished a delightful dinner in a lovely dining room, and afterward sat on the terrace and gaped at the stars. It's only 9:45 pm, but we want to get to bed so we can get an early start tomorrow. I'm presently sitting at a quaint little antique desk, just soaking up the sounds of crickets and enjoying the fresh clean air. The open window looks across Sun Moon Lake.

After writing the above, I turned out the light, and would you believe – a full moon was beginning to throw its light over the top of the mountain straight across from me. I sat there about half an hour watching it rise and shine across the lake. WOW !!!!!!!!!!!!!!!!!

Sunday May 24, 1970

Today we took a boat ride across the lake to what was supposed to be an Aborigine Village, but it was quite commercial. Returning to the Hotel I met a group of Vietnamese ARVN officers. It was really interesting to visit with them as they were in Taiwan for several weeks learning "Psychological Warfare". They will return to Vietnam and as they put it, "work in POW Camps and brainwash the Viet Cong". They were absolutely amazed when they learned I was working in Vietnam. Later Millie and I returned to Taipei by train, and didn't arrive until midnight.

Monday May 25, 1970

Today was a full day. Millie and I visited the National Palace Museum and in the evening attended a Chinese Opera. Although we couldn't understand anything that was happening, it was quite interesting. We've been sampling all kinds of Chinese food as we go along. Last night, it was Mongolian Barbeque. You pick out your own sliced meat, put in some shredded cabbage, add your own seasoning and they mix it up and throw it on an open charcoal grill. It's good, but my favorite has been Cantonese food.

Tuesday May 26, 1970

Today, Kay and I got up at 6:00 a.m. and went on a Tour to Toroko Gorge. There were seven of us from the R&R Center plus our guide. We flew there in a China Airways plane, and then took a bus through the gorge, which winds 12 miles through mountains of solid marble. Why this place isn't more famous astounds me because it is truly a spectacle.

We had lunch at a lovely restaurant. All of us dined at a round table full of delicious Cantonese food. It was real homey. We joined up with another group, so there were eleven Americans at our round table, and a full second table of Orientals. The guide had to repeat everything in English, Chinese, and Japanese. Our last stop on the tour, after watching some folk dances, was a visit to the marble factory. We saw huge marble stones being cut and polished. It takes four days for one rock. I purchased two marble vases, and some green marble book-ends.

Having just returned to the Hotel, I'm bushed. Kay, who I have been traveling with, is an interesting person. She's like Mary in that she has a daughter about 22 years old. Her father escaped from Russia and her mother is from Puerto Rico.

Well, I better start packing up my gear because we leave very early tomorrow. You know, Mom, at least half the fun of these trips is in knowing how much you enjoy them along with me, both in spirit and through the pictures. Love, Bette

June 2, 1970

Col. Lawrence had his Change of Command on Thursday, and then stayed in Qui Nhon for three days. He took Mary and I out for Lobster dinner, and we had a real nice time. He's such a fascinating person. I think I mentioned earlier that he was taking over 5th Special Forces. Mary completed her Qui Nhon tour, Sunday night, and we haven't received a third staff person yet to take her place.

I met another nice person this week. He's with an advisory team and their living quarters are on the beach. He invited me over to go swimming and have dinner.

We also went to dinner last night with Alice and her friend. This morning I woke up very nauseated so I called Alice to work for me, but they are also sick. Doc Butcher came by and gave me a shot and said he thinks we have a slight case of food poisoning. He was also kind enough to help me deal with a case of shingles and I am much better now. Love you, Bette.

June 6, 1970

Mary has been gone six days now, and we still haven't had any word about a replacement, but Alice and I are getting along just fine.

The other night I went with a friend to dinner accompanied by a Vietnamese Colonel and his wife. We ate at a Chinese restaurant in downtown Qui Nhon.

Got to run... I'm really busy these days, but still enjoy my work immensely. More later – Love, Bette

P.S. Mom, a little gift is on the way that I picked up in Taiwan.

June 17, 1970

I got your nice long letter yesterday and I'm so glad that you and the family are enjoying my R&R's through my letters and pictures. Mary's been gone two weeks now, and still no word of a replacement. It actually hasn't been that bad because we have such a good night crew of GI's and we can let them close up at 11:00 p.m. Next week, Alice goes on R&R and I'll work 7:00 a.m. to 7:00 p.m. every day, but everything is running smoothly.

Once or twice a week I've been going to the beach house where the Advisory Engineer group is stationed. I'm treated like one of the family now, so they asked me to make potato salad. You wouldn't believe how they raved about it. Everybody went back for seconds, and even two Vietnamese girls who were guests said they really liked it. All I did was chop it up and season it, because the egg and potatoes were already boiled. I didn't even have celery and onion, but I think that's why some of the men liked it. I sure enjoy my visits there because not only is the beach atmosphere relaxing but every night they show an outdoor movie and I get to swing in a hammock to watch it. That's where I'm going tomorrow on my day off.

Since Mary left, Alice has moved into the adjoining room, leaving me a room to myself temporarily. Alice's boyfriend got it closed off and air conditioned for me, so I'm fixing it up, and it will sure be nice. I moved in a little two-seater sofa and coffee table, making it so much homier. I've also had a small refrigerator for some time now.

Got to get this in the mail, so by for now. Love, Bette

June 21, 1970
It's now 5:15 p.m. Sunday evening and after a pretty hectic day things have finally quieted down.

Alice has left for Taipei, and I'm here running the whole show. I'm actually not nervous about it, because we have so many friends I could call on if I need them. Even the airfield commander comes by every afternoon for a milk and ice cream float I fix especially for him. I work from 7:00 a.m. to 7:00 p.m. and then the GI's take over till 11:00 p.m.

I'm still writing to Vince and he even mentions meeting me on an R&R in Hawaii, but as much as I care for him, I just don't think it will work out. It's strange that I feel that way, because he'll make someone a great husband.

Speaking of R&R's, here's my latest brainstorm!!! You know my 30 day leave is coming up soon – well, I learned the R&R Center in Australia has numerous families who wish to take in Americans who are on R&R. Therefore, I'm going to write the R&R Office and see if there is any possibility of staying with a family on a ranch during my leave. All the GI's I've talked to say that the people are unbelievably friendly, and go out of their way for Americans. It would be expensive because I will have to pay my own way wherever I go on leave. I think to Australia it's about $600.00 round trip. I've already seen most of the places near-by, and I think I'd enjoy getting out of the orient for a while and seeing something different. What do you think?

Just now a pilot friend of mine came in and gave me the name of a family in Australia he stayed with, who he said were delightful... Gee, I get excited just thinking about it. Boy, could I stand a good ole horseback ride.

Well, that's about it for now. Stay happy!

P.S. Did I tell you I only spent $140.00 on my R&R to Taipei?

June 25, 1970

Honestly, if you have your health you have everything... I visited the hospital yesterday. One Sgt. I was talking to last weekend who had just been dismissed from the hospital, went back to the field and four days later he's back with another gunshot wound. What's ironic is his friend from the same platoon was also shot and they wound up in the same ward. His buddy went back to the field, and a couple days later he too was critically injured.

Lt. Ken Slaughter, is leading their platoon now, and they have lost about half of their men in the last two weeks. A GI was brought to the 67th Evac last night who was near a grenade when it exploded. He witnessed his buddy's arm get nearly blown off, and he died of shock without even getting a scratch.

I'm kind of proud of myself because Alice has been gone five days now and the USO Club is still standing. Ha! We've had several problems arise, but nothing I couldn't handle.

I spoke with the Saigon Office today and I think Gerry is coming down from Da Nang to be with us. She was here before and the USO staff like her a lot. She's about Mary's age, and I'm glad to know she's coming.

I felt honored the other night because Col. Stewart, the Airfield Commander, invited me to dinner with him, a WAC major, and the Commander of Lane Airfield. Col. Stewart, was a friend of Mary's, and when she left, I think he sort of adopted me. He fixed steaks, lobster, baked potato, and salad. It sure was delicious.

I'm so glad, Mom, that you taught me to accept people as just, people, regardless of station in life, color, religion, or anything else. It allows me to relax and just be myself, without any put-on or pretense. I've never found it to go wrong. I was honored not so much by their position, but all three are quite a bit older than I am, like late 40's and early 50's, and yet I thoroughly enjoyed the evening.

Chaplain Mathis told me Tan Son Nhut USO caught a grenade in the kitchen a couple days ago, but only one cook was slightly hurt. I think I forgot to tell you, on May 19th, we were in another mortar attack which was the night before I left for R&R. Mary and I spent a half hour under the mattress again. Camp Granite got some rockets since then, but only a few received minor wounds. It could have been real serious because one rocket landed directly where they were showing the movie, but it was the second round, and after the 1st round hit everyone scattered.

Tank Farm Two had about 11 zappers barge through the front gate with satchel charges. Seven GI's were killed and four burned beyond recognition. I drive right by there on my way to the Valley picking up supplies.

Also, about four nights ago, some GI's from North English were in a truck bringing prostitutes from town out to the LZ. They used very poor judgment traveling the road that late and "Charlie" took advantage of the situation. VC shot up the truck something fierce, and knowing they didn't have a chance the GI's ran and got away. The girl up front in the cab got away uninjured. Two girls were shot, and "Charlie" threw a "Molotov Cocktail" into the back of the truck.

I don't know why I'm telling you all this except that sometimes it feels so great just to be alive; especially when you have so many blessings. I love you, Bette

July 5, 1970

Thanks much for sending the goodies. I'm glad you all approve of my forthcoming trip. Actually things have been very exciting right here in "Qui Nhon by the Sea". You won't even believe my latest adventures.

Last week there was a party in our quadrangle that is now all fixed up with paint, plants, and lawn furniture. My good friend, Jim Wilson, the Veterinarian, pointed out an extremely handsome, black haired, Irish civilian and began telling me about him. Jim referred to him as "Super Spy", and said he had been in Special Forces, fought in South America, and was now a mercenary here in Nam.

Well, as you can imagine, my interest span reached a high pitch. I saw him again one night at a party, and the following day he stopped by the USO and invited me out for dinner. All he said was he would pick me up at 6:30 pm. He arrived in civilian clothes, driving a jeep, and wearing a gun as usual. As it turned out he had prepared baked potatoes, salad, and put two delicious steaks on the grill after we arrived. There are five members in the organization he works with which is pacification and security, something or other. It's all very secretive.

They own two houses in downtown Qui Nhon, surrounded by high barbed wire fences, with Chinese guards surrounding the place. I swear it's just like in a movie. Well anyway, he's 27, single, and of course a playboy, although not what I consider a "typical playboy". He's extremely intelligent as far as world affairs are concerned, and to put it mildly he's a fascinating person. I've seen him several times this week, and each time I figure it will be the last because there are lots of girls around that he's been dating.

I could never get serious about someone like him, but it sure is a comfortable and fun relationship. Today, he stopped by in his jungle fatigues after coming back from a mission. He has teams of Vietnamese and they capture top NVA and VC officials as far as I can figure out. Jim told me that Super Spy was forced to move out of several locations because he had such a high price on his head. Super Spy has mentioned that the type of small, specialty units, like the one he works with, is how jungle warfare should be fought. He recommends that tactic, rather than deploying a large number of troops with lots of heavy equipment. I guess that pretty well wraps up the latest events. Love you bunches, Bette

July 18, 1970
It was great visiting with you the other day on the USO phone. It was like I haven't been gone at all.

I was so pleased to get the two pictures of "my Mamoo". She still looks great.

I'm sending pictures of a girl in a wheel chair. I brought her situation to the attention of Doc. Butcher and Chaplain Hall. She has been living in a back room at the orphanage without being able to get around because she is too heavy for the staff to move. The Chaplain wrote to his friend in Oklahoma who sent the wheel chair for her. This will greatly improve her life.

I still have a few dates with "Super Spy", and now I have dinner occasionally with a dust-off pilot, who is happily married, but very nice company. Many of my male friends in Nam have wonderful families and it seems like they are more mature, and it's easier for us to have meaningful conversations. It's very difficult for them to be away so long from loved-ones, especially under such stressful conditions.

Well, I best run. Take care…much love, Bette

Wheel chair donation is life-changing for orphan

Thursday July 23, 1970

Just as I sat down to dry my hair and write this letter I was invited by Jim, the Veterinarian, to eat lobster with the group who live in the Quad. The guys have fixed up our quadrangle real nice and now there are parties, cookouts, and volleyball games. The grass is green, the plants are thriving and it's all painted bright colors.

Unfortunately for many, life is not so gay and carefree. I'm sad to tell you, that yesterday Lt. Slaughter was killed. I'm sure you'll remember. He's the sweet guy I visited in the hospital every day for a week when he had malaria. I also pinned on his 1st Lt. bar at the "dining-in" at North English. His 21st birthday was about three days ago, and in two weeks he was going to Hawaii to get married. Ken had already spent his time in the field, but had to return to take the place of another Lt. who was killed. He was leading his men on a patrol, saw two VC, went after them and tripped off a booby trap. He lost an arm, a leg, and died four minutes later in the arms of Chaplain Mathis, his good friend who happened to be in the area.

It was strange how I learned about it. I called the hospital Liaison Officer to get a ride for a Captain and, Sgt. Dillard said, "Hey Bette, you've got some guys to visit over here from 4th Battalion." He said, a Lt. is in Ward 6 and a Lt. from Alpha Co. was killed. I hung up the phone knowing it must be Ken. Sitting in my office at the time was, Capt. Bill Prout, with the 173rd, and oddly enough Ken's driver, Rudy, a PFC who always stopped in to see me with Lt Slaughter. Rudy was just returning from R&R.

Chaplain Mathis was supposed to meet me for dinner last night because his tour has ended, and he's on his way home. Instead he met Bill, Gerry, and I at the USO. He and Ken were very close friends, so he's going to stop by and see Ken's folks back in the states. After dinner the four of us were visiting on the quad patio, and the siren went off for a practice red alert. It wound up that Bill and the chaplain stayed in a room at the Quad, with Bill sleeping on the floor.

How very strange, is life and death in Vietnam. I've never lost any friends before, and I keep thinking how glad I am now, that I took a little time to see Lt. Slaughter when he was in the hospital with malaria. I even sent him a poster to brighten up his bunker. It's so important to enjoy and appreciate people while you can.

Well, another Chapter ends. Life will be a little different now that all our friends from North English have gone. Please take care. I love you all very much, Bette

July 30, 1970

Just a line to tell you how thrilled I am with my new clothes. Everything fits fine. There was a party the night the first box arrived so I wore my pretty yellow dress and got lots of compliments. I can't get over you two being able to shop for me and having everything fit so well. Thank you bunches!!!

When the packages came Mary was here visiting and she was anxious to see everything. There were several others in the office too so we all got a big kick out of opening the boxes. It was like back home when we would get excited over someone getting something new.

Yesterday we had a fun trip. Gerry and I took a steak cookout up to Hill 474. It's located outside of North English. The hill is real high so you can see the valley and all the way to the coast. There were 15 guys stationed on the hill and choppers flew in 7 other GI's for the meal. You've never seen a more appreciative bunch. This one kid they called Doc was so thrilled with his apple that after two bites, he held it out and took a picture of it! Bless his heart...

I shopped at the PX today and bought a cassette and am/fm radio combination. It was $50.00 and I got it from the store manager for $31.00 because it had been repaired. It looks brand new. Over here you can buy blank tapes for 80 cents and tape off of everyone else's tapes. By the time I get home I should have a pretty good tape library. I was going to get a big one by Panasonic for $150.00. It's stereo and has two speakers, but I'd have to place a special order for it. You get some real good buys over here on equipment like that.

Today our mama son informed me she will have to quit because she only has two rooms in the quad to take care of now, and that's not enough to feed her four children. Her husband was killed by the VC several years ago, and she is the sole support of her family. She said she hasn't been able to pay her rent for three months. It's 3,000 P a month and that's all she's been getting paid. I guess she's been using that money for food. Her house is just one room for the five of them.

Honestly, I don't know why life is so good to some, and such a struggle for others. She lay on my bed and cried because she hates to leave us. I'm going to try and get her a job at the USO, or write a letter and get her a job at the Depot.

Well, that's all for now. Take care and be happy, for we have so much to be thankful for. Love, Belle

Cookout in the field

August 7, 1970

Mom, I just got your note saying, you're starting your vacation. I sure hope you have a nice time.

Yesterday was my day off, and I had a lovely time. A dust-off pilot friend of ours took me to the leprosarium. A medevac chopper flew us over and landed right on the beach. The flight is only a couple minutes out of Qui Nhon, just over the mountain.

I truly love that place. It's always so peaceful there. We stayed on the beach for three and a half hours and I got just enough sun. Then last night there was a cookout in the Quad. All in all it was a very nice day.

Alice is leaving today and will be gone for two weeks. I got a nice letter and some brochures about Australia. I'm really looking forward to my trip. Well, it's 7:10 a.m. and I have a busy day ahead. I just wanted to say hello.

Well, lets see what this chapter will include. Doc Butcher has gone home. He had to leave early due to a family emergency.

Recently I met an officer with the 593rd Support Command. They have a small club right on the beach. Last night we went there for a movie, some pizza and wine, and then relaxed on the patio overlooking the ocean. He graduated from West Point and is very interesting.

Let's see, what else exciting happened this weekend? I went out to the Leprosarium to pick up a truckload of tile for the USO kitchen. Patients make the tile, and it's lovely. I also visited the shop where they have old wooden looms for weaving. I'm looking forward to tomorrow when some of us are invited out there for lunch with Mother Superior. I think, Jim Wilson, the veterinarian, will attend to some of their animals. The nuns are French and I've heard all about the fantastic meals they serve.

On August 17th, Miss America will have a USO Show in the hanger across the street from our USO Club.

Love you much, Bette

August 18, 1970

Yesterday was quite a day! From 7:00 a.m. to 7:00 p.m. we had a door count of over 2,000.

The Miss America Show was in the hangar across the street and convoys were even brought in from the valley to see the program. I got to see most of the show, but wandered around a little and talked to some of the guys who couldn't get up close enough to see. The girls were lovely. I liked Miss California and Miss Colorado. I can't say I envy them at all because I've been treated like Miss America for the past twelve months. Did you know I had my "one year in-country" anniversary Sunday?

Oh, the most fun thing I've done lately was going to the leprosarium last week. Jim, the Veterinarian, two nurses, a dust-off pilot and I were invited for lunch. Boy, was it exquisite! We had soup, salad and gorgeous fat shrimp. That was followed by a course of chicken and pork, French fries, wine, and for desert a pineapple pound cake soaked in (something), and delicious custard. Wow!!! We dined on a little patio surrounded by beautiful vines of bougainvillea. Afterward we walked passed lovely white statues as we made our way to the white sandy cove to swim. Guess that's all the "rap" for now.

P.S. Just a quick note to say I did get to see three of the Miss America team yesterday. They came to the Club for a quick tour. I got to visit with Miss Colorado for about 5 minutes. (Funny, but they seem like any other girls to me...) Ha! Six of us, including, Margo, the PR lady from the Saigon Office, went out to eat at the Seaman's Club last night.

Oh, another sidelight! I met the cutest guy from Dallas who dates Miss

Texas Appaloosa. He has done real well riding in rodeos in Texas. His dad owns an Arabian Ranch outside of Dallas.

Got to go now…I love you bunches, Bette

Sunday August 30, 1970

This is a hot Sunday afternoon, and there have been a few moments of quiet in the office allowing me time to say hello. I'm sure the temperature has been well over 100 degrees for several weeks now, but you never hear a weather report, so you just know it's hot. Thank goodness our office is air-conditioned.

Yesterday, I went to the Leprosarium with, a young, good-looking Cobra Fighter Pilot.

There have been days lately, I must admit, when I get a little depressed because I know the day is coming soon when I'll have to decide again which road to take when my tour is completed. Freedom and having responsibility only for myself, is great most of the time, but there are moments too when it would be nice to have some roots. Every person I know who is single seems to agree.

Well, enough gab for now…

Take care and know I love you all dearly, Bette

September 4, 1970

Last night I went to the movie and saw, the "Hell Fighters". I never watch TV, but each ward in the Hospital has one, and the programs don't look very interesting.

A week ago I took sundaes to a GI who has lost his leg. I told him he needed fattening up. Mom, you would be amazed at how some of these guys accept the loss of a limb. He was just great, and wants to send me a picture when he's walking on his "funny foot" as he calls it.

They had another real bad booby trap hit last weekend out of North English. Seven guys were hurt real bad. One GI died immediately, and another lost both legs and an arm. To some people it sounds like the war is over. Things around Qui Nhon have been pretty quiet, but then I talk to guys out in the field…

Na Trang was attacked at 7:00 a.m. the other day, and two barracks were hit. I just wonder what kind of reports you are getting at home.

Well, I better get to work now. Eleven days till Australia. Love you much, Bette

September 12, 1970

Only four more days and I'll be on my way! I will be staying in
Singapore a day or two on my way to Sydney. I'll leave Qui Nhon the 15th
and Saigon the 16th. I hope to stay with a family the first couple of weeks,
maybe book tours for a week, and then relax in Sydney.

I wish I could put in words just how I feel after being in Nam for 13
months. Lately, I've found myself missing the little things, which are
really big things. For instance, there are very few birds in Qui Nhon.
When you do hear one sing, it's a big treat. There aren't any flowers and
only a few scrawny trees because the area has been defoliated. The ocean
can be beautiful, but it is extremely polluted, and in certain areas, the
smell is overwhelming. I also miss the sight of a happy normal family, if
there is such a thing anymore.

You see, over here, on the streets one sees mostly prostitutes and elderly
men and women. Bunches of children run wild, playing in the garbage
lining the roads. Yesterday, there was a big fire near the compound where
we live. A very dear Vietnamese friend who works at the USO said, as fast
as people could get their few possessions outside and go in for more, they
were stolen.

Don't get me wrong though, Mom. Good things are happening all the
time...Yesterday, Tony, a little orphaned Vietnamese boy who has been
hanging around with American GI's for several years, flew to Da Lot with
some pilots and brought me back a beautiful red rose. I have many friends
here, and I always feel so good when they make a special point to drop by
the USO and see me when they come in from the field.

I won't have a permanent address in Australia, so don't try to write. The
R&R Center in Sydney will know my whereabouts. Till later, Bette

September 18, 1970

Hi ducks!

Well, I'm on my way to the land down under...Our 707 Boeing Jet left
Singapore at 9:00 p.m. (one hour late), and we are due to arrive in Sydney
at 7:30 a.m. I'm sitting next to a lovely couple from New Zealand, so it's
bound to be a pleasant flight. Last night I had dinner alone in the beautiful
hotel restaurant. I guess the young waiter felt sorry for me because he
invited me to go on a tour of Singapore. At breakfast, I sat next to a
Chinese fellow who works for the airlines and he also invited to show
me around. Therefore, I got to see the reservoir and park; the Botanic
Gardens; Tiger Balm Gardens and the Museum.

Singapore has three major races: Chinese, Malayans, and Indians. Their government is equally interracial. The Chinese and Indians are mostly well educated, and speak at least two or three languages. They are a very ambitious people resulting in a very modern city, which is exceptionally clean. (No wonder, since there is a $500.00 fine for littering).

I bought myself a "Sarong Kabaya", which is the native dress of the Malays and is seen all over Singapore. I just thought it would be fun to have. I stayed in a very nice hotel, the Singapura. It was $45.00 a night Singapore ($15 U.S.). In Sydney I'll look for something much less elaborate.

We are soon going to land in Djakarta, and it's getting a little bumpy, so by till later. (We won't be getting off; there is just a 45minute stopover).

Monday September 21, 1970
My first day in Sydney, I went straight to the R&R Center to see about staying with a family. They made the arrangements, and while there I met an American GI on R&R. He took me to the Zoo by way of a ferry, and later we went out to dinner.

The next morning, Sunday, I took the 7:15 a.m. plane to Kempsey, New South Wales, where I am now staying with the Smyth family. They have a daughter 24, one 20, and a son 15. They own 360 acres and raise dairy and beef cattle, and sheep. This reminds me so much of farm families back home.

The only drawback is the weather. I've been absolutely freezing. It's only down in the 50's but I'm used to 110 degrees. My one salvation is a gift I found on my desk before leaving Vietnam. It was from a thoughtful young GI who comes to the USO for some of the programs. He had just returned from R&R and knew I was leaving. It's a lovely wool slip over sweater with a note saying, "you'll need this in Australia". Well, I certainly have. Right now my hand is so cold I can hardly write this letter. Jenny, one of the daughters, is sitting here in her bare feet with the doors and window open. Oh well, I'm sure I'll survive. They have horses, in fact a new colt was born this morning. I hope we get to ride. More later, Bette

The Smyth family in Australia offered their home and hospitality to many arriving from Vietnam for rest and recuperation (R&R)

October 6, 1970

At this time I'm on an R&R flight and we just left Darwin Australia. I was lucky to get a seat, so now I'll get my return commercial ticket refunded. It meant I had to cut my leave short about a week, but to tell you the truth I'm quite ready to go back to Nam. I had a wonderful time and got to do everything I wanted. My round trip ticket was $627.00, and I'll get about half of that back. In addition to that I spent about $440.00. I bought several dresses for work, and of course meals and hotel bills add up, plus the plane ticket from Sydney to Kempsey.

After leaving the Smyth family in Kempsey, I went back to Sydney, and shopped for about three days. I stayed at the YWCA because it was close to downtown and across the street from Hyde Park. I would shop all day, go to a small café for dinner, and then walk downtown to a movie. I saw

"Butch Cassidy and the Sundance Kid", "Airport" and "MASH". All three were very good.

Did I mention in the post card about the dance the Smyth family took me to in Kempsey? It was a formal dance held in the country with a live band. It was so interesting because they dance to old Australian folk songs that are rather formal, but lots of fun. Young and old couples took part. I think, Mr. Smyth, and half the community, were trying to get me married off to a 35-year-old bachelor who owns a ranch. I danced with him a lot, but wound up being taken home by a very nice fellow whose parents have both died, leaving him to care for his 12-year-old brother. On my last day there I got a phone call from Mrs. Melville who arranged my stay with the Smyth family. She asked if I would call a friend of hers in Sydney, because he had an American boy working with him at the newspaper, and he was very concerned about him. He said Ted's wife had recently left him, and he thought seeing an American girl, and having someone to talk to would help.

After several days of shopping I decided to call and he put Ted on the phone. He in turn, invited me to spend the long Holiday weekend with him in Canberra, the Australian capital.

We had dinner Thursday night, and Friday left by car for about a five-hour trip. Ted has lived in Australia for six years, and had been married just 8 months, when his wife left with another man. Ted is nice, and I thoroughly enjoyed his friends. We stayed with his best friend and his wife who have an 8-month-old baby. Then we visited Ted's sister and her friends who each have small children. Sunday we all went on a picnic and enjoyed a delicious barbeque meal by a lovely river. It was a very relaxed day and I thoroughly enjoyed it. We had (on a picnic mind you), crackers and Swiss cheese, fried sausages, salad, steak and even wine.

Monday we all went to the horse races then Ted and I drove back to Sydney. I guess I'm just not use to the highway, but I was a nervous wreck the whole trip. The traffic was real thick and we were in a Volkswagen. Driving on the left side of the road with the driver on the right was the final blow.

I'll take flying in helicopters over Charlie country anytime! Ha! All is well now, and I'm sure looking forward to seeing my friends in Nam again. After all this traveling, I might be ready to stay close to home in the USA for a while. We'll see - All my love, Bette

When my tour in Nam was over, Mom admitted the only time she really worried about me was during the time I spent on R&R in Australia. I

*wrote home less often and she felt there was no US government there to
see about me in an emergency.*

October 10, 1970

Just a quick line before I go to the post office. I got back to Qui Nhon
Oct. 7th. As I walked across the Airfield from the plane, one of the guys in
the tower said, "Welcome home Bette"! It sure made me feel good. Then
Col. Stewart, the Airfield Commander happened to be there and he carried
my bag and gave me a ride home.

I learned there was some pretty heavy action that took place while I was
away. One night there were 19 incoming rounds that hit all around our
quad. One round hit the little PX and even the Officer's Club. My car got a
rock thrown into the windshield.

Got to run now. Everything looks so pretty and green before the real
monsoon starts. The weather is still nice with bits of rain now and then.

P.S. I have one favor to ask. Would one of you mind calling the
Governor's Office or the VFW and see if I could get some free "Okie
pens" to give out to the guys for Christmas. Got to run now. Love you all,
Bette

October 27, 1970

I was sure glad to see a letter from you today. I'm in real good spirits, but
it looks like the monsoon has started all in one day. There is a typhoon off
the coast and we are getting high winds and lots of steady rain. It's nice to
be inside where it's dry and cozy.

I decorated the USO Club for Halloween the other night and we have
little paper pumpkins on all the tables. The big one you sent last year is
on the reception desk. Lots of troops are moving through here on their
way home. They opened up Camp Granite again to house the 4th Infantry
Division on their way back to the states. That means we get a lot of fellas
in transit, and I enjoy helping them get a place to stay etc. The other
night I was locking up and found five guys standing on the patio, the rain
pouring down and they didn't know where to go because the transit billets
were all full. I finally got them beds at the hospital.

I've been seeing two guys on and off, and the other night I wound up
going to dinner with both. In the last month one of them lost whole crews
in seven major accidents, and of course, he really takes it hard. We've
been going to dinner at a lovely club overlooking the ocean. They also
show a movie every night.

Alice has been gone for almost two weeks. She's staying with the guy

115

she's dating in Saigon, and they also went to Singapore.

I'm glad you all are fixing up the house and planning a big Thanksgiving Well, that's all the gab for now. I'm so thrilled to see Mamoo's letters and know that she is well. All my love, Bette

November 6, 1970

I guess you probably read about the floods we've been having. They didn't damage the Club or our hooch, but a lot of places were washed away and many Vietnamese left homeless. A lot of the chopper pilots were out picking up people off rooftops.

Well, guess whose a TV personality now? I had my debut yesterday. Ron, the fellow I did the radio show with is doing TV now, and asked me to do a 15minute interview. It was taped yesterday morning and shown in the afternoon. Ron simply asked questions regarding the USO and how this job has affected me. I'm surprised at how relaxed I felt. I also enjoyed the ride up to the top of the mountain. All this time and I've never been up their with it's fantastic view of Qui Nhon.

Today, we went to the 67th Evac hospital with ice cream sundaes as we do every Friday. I met one GI in intensive care who has been there three weeks, and has several to go before they can safely medevac him out of Vietnam. He was hit in the heart by a booby trap. I learned it is his birthday, so I gathered up several presents to take him. Last month we served 1,050 patients as a result of these weekly hospital visits.
Love you, Bette

November 11, 1970

There are some things that just can't be explained in letters, so let it suffice to say that the last three months have been extra special. I engaged in a relationship with someone knowing that it was only temporary, but I was ready to enjoy every minute while it lasted. It has come to an end, and I'm still exuberant. His best friend and I joined him on a helicopter champagne flight to an air base where he will leave for home. He earned great respect from those men who worked with him. It was the perfect way to say goodbye and oh, so romantic. I've had so many experiences that most people don't have in a lifetime. I've been truly blessed...

Mom, don't worry about sending me anything for Christmas, because it will be such a short time before I pack up to go home. I'm so thankful you are all well and happy.

Please know that I am too. Much love always, Bette

November 16, 1970

Today is another cool, windy day with some rain, and we are expecting another typhoon tonight only smaller than the last.

I just spoke with, Frazier, the personnel director, in the Saigon office. He asked if I would consider extending in Nam for a few months before accepting a Pacific or European assignment. I told him I would rather go home for a while first, but I would think it over. Everything here is changing so rapidly with the troops moving out, and we sort of expect the action to step up quite a bit, but that remains to be seen. I received the Okie pins, so please thank whoever is responsible for sending them. I only have one left.

Tonight, Alice and I are going to the valley where the Korean Rock Tiger Division is stationed.

Wednesday, Alice, Millie and Margot from Saigon, and I are (weather permitting) going to take 100 steaks up to an artillery base for a cook-in (under a tarp probably).

Oh, by the way, Alice broke her engagement. She decided she's just not ready to settle down. He offered her everything, but she found she just wasn't in love with him. You wouldn't believe the experiences we have over here as far as interpersonal relationships. I just wonder how much I have changed. It will be interesting to see, and anyway, I know you and Bid will get a kick out of the stories.

I'll be thinking about you during Thanksgiving. We do indeed have so much to be thankful for.

Each day is a whole new adventure! Love, Bette

November 17, 1970

I wanted to write this down before I forget the details. Last night Alice and I were invited to the Korean Rock Tiger Division for a special dinner. Alice is dating an officer now, who must personally know the top brass. The dinner was held at the home of one of the Korean officers, and there were nine of us present. Would you believe two Korean Generals and three Colonels. They prepared a fantastic meal served Korean style, (sitting on the floor). The meal began by breaking a raw egg into a bowl, (one for each of us); to which we added, soy sauce, sugar, and then stirred. This was used as a dipping bowl for the remaining food. The main course was cooked in a pan right on the table. It had cabbage; carrots; onions, and beef.

In addition, there were little plates scattered all over the table containing: bean sprouts; greens; fish of all kinds including squid, and of course kimchi (which is fermented cabbage with a hot hot sauce on it).

We also had sake to drink and beer. Their custom is to toast each other, and then finish off the glass. They teased me because I ate so much, but it wasn't filling at all. The last thing served was seaweed soup, which was delicious, and a big bowl of rice. After dinner we listened to Korean music, and Alice and I danced with all the Koreans. We were the only American girls they have had visit Tiger Town except for one lady major, so they enjoyed it as much as we did. We were given a pin worn by the Tiger Division and also a pretty gold necklace with a fish on it.

The only hitch in the evening was an incident involving an American officer following dinner. His actions were extremely inappropriate and you'd think he would know better. I guess sake got the best of him. I was stunned at being in that particular situation and felt quite vulnerable since we were miles away from Qui Nhon. Nobody else was around, but I kept my cool and insisted on being left alone. In retrospect, I feel like someone had given him false expectations of what the evening would involve. Days later I found a written apology attached to my door.

This incident stands out because nearly 100% of the time I was treated with the utmost respect by the troops. I even felt perfectly safe picking up GI's carrying their M-16's who needed a ride somewhere. It saddens me greatly to now hear numerous news reports of how women in the military are often treated.

Yesterday we had a tremendous field trip. Alice and I took steaks to 100 guys at an Artillery Base, LZ Salem. Millie, who broadcasts the "USO Showtime Radio" program, came with us to tape her show and take pictures. We arrived at a perfect time because 30 men were going on a raid today, taking two howitzers up north to the An Do Valley. There were six sections at the post and each had a howitzer. They shot off all of them as a demonstration for us. I had been invited by several of the GI's who stopped by the USO, and they were so pleased that we came. They were also very nervous about the upcoming raid because the majority of them are new "in country".

Well, I've got to get back to work. Love you much, Bette

November 28, 1970

I've felt especially close to home this last week picturing all of you together, and the big turkey cooking all day. I was going to call home on the 25th, but the connections weren't good and I thought that would be pretty frustrating. We served a free turkey buffet at work and Alice made some pumpkin pies.

After Christmas do you realize how short the time is before I'll be home? (Yes, I guess you do...)

Well, there isn't much news. Just Hi, and I love ya lots, Bette

December 3, 1970

It was so good to get your letter today, Mom, telling about Thanksgiving and Johnny's Christmas present. That's just great! Maybe I'll retire and just sit home and watch color TV. I got so tickled at you telling about Mamoo being concerned that I might not stay with USO. At this point I'm fairly sure I will, someplace anyway. I keep meeting guys from Oklahoma who tell me I wouldn't even recognize Oklahoma City. I guess with urban renewal it has developed a lot. Is the Mummer's Theater finished yet?

Last night Gerry fell and broke four ribs. I had to call our good friend, the Flight Surgeon, Dr. Jim Rogers, at 4:00 am to see what I could give her for the pain. Jim is a wonderful person. He's planning on doing his residency in Stockton, California.

Today I took her to the hospital for X-Rays and she will have to spend several days in bed.

Did I tell you that a colonel wanted me to meet his son who was visiting from down near Saigon? He brought his son by twice to meet me and I was gone both times. Boy – how my luck runs sometimes.

Today is a cloudy afternoon, and I just put out a whole bunch of homemade cookies that someone sent for the guys. We are getting the Christmas decorations ready, and I'll probably put them out tomorrow. I'll also be getting out the little tree for my room. Enclosed are two pictures the Smyth family sent me from Australia.

Well, I better sign-off. Take care and know that I love y'all bunches, Bette

December 10, 1970

Well, I imagine right now you are wondering where I am, and how bad the situation really is in Qui Nhon. We made Paul Harvey News so I'm sure you've heard about it.

I didn't get to go on R&R because we have been so busy. It's a good thing considering the following events. First of all, Alice took the USO report to Saigon, and has been stranded there for three days. That left Gerry and me, with her four broken ribs, so she couldn't work a full shift.

Monday, in the late afternoon, we heard that a young Vietnamese boy had been accidentally shot in the head by an American GI, and the whole town was going crazy. The boy was a student, and the incident occurred near his school. Everyone got involved, and it really snowballed, with Charlie's help, I'm sure. They put the boy's body in a casket, and drove it all over town telling what happened.

About that time someone yelled, "come and see this bus"! I went outside and there was an Air Force bus that was coming back from Phu Cat. It was completely bashed in. The two front windows were gone, and half of the others. We also began hearing many stories from GI's coming into the USO who said they had been mobbed and stoned as they came through town. Soon after, the entire airfield went on yellow alert, the gates were closed, and nobody was allowed to leave. The next day people continued demonstrating and marching, so the traffic was again stopped.

Alice was still in Saigon, and Gerry was at home over at Quincy Compound, so I couldn't leave the airfield and she couldn't leave over there. Fortunately for me, a friend lives on the airfield, so I was invited to stay with him, and two of his co-workers. I began to feel like I was living in a men's dorm...

By the end of the second day, I still couldn't leave and my clothes were grubby, so my friends at dust-off sent me some clean clothes in a chopper, would you believe. I couldn't fly back to Quincy because I had to open the Club early the next day.

All in all, I had a great time! Then yesterday, only six of our Vietnamese staff showed up for work because the mayor put the town on a 24-hour curfew. Of all days we were swamped with GI's, so I dipped ice cream and made milkshakes. (We always knew my waitress experience would be helpful). The situation is about the same today, but at least we can drive back and forth.

Today, I met a GI from your hometown, Ada, Oklahoma. About 10 minutes later he came to the office with a bag of shelled pecans. They sure will be good on ice cream sundaes. I'm not even sorry about not going on R&R because I was really needed here, and besides it's been fun.

Oh! Two friends came over last week and helped Gerry and I decorate my little tree. It looks so pretty. I also decorated the Club and it looks nice too. Love you much, Bette

December 17, 1970
We have had a little excitement since I've written to you last.
On Monday, we were told to expect the President of World Airways and about 35 people from Saigon. They came in on a special flight, so we

drove all three of our USO cars out on the runway to meet them. It just so happened that they brought a surprise guest, Fess Parker, or (Daniel Boone). Mr. Parker, was introduced to us by our director in Saigon. Then they began unloading live Christmas trees; boxes of beautiful decorations; and several frozen turkeys, all donated by the President of World Airways. Fess being a good friend of his, had joined him on the trip to visit all the USO Clubs. I have to say, Fess Parker, is just as big, good looking, and warm-hearted as you see him on TV. Calling each of us by name the whole time he was here really left a good impression. He stayed for over an hour, playing the piano, a game of pool, and visiting with all the GI's. It was really a treat!

Do you realize, I've been "in country" for 16 months. It won't be long now before I'm home. I'm anxious to see everyone even though I hate to see this tour come to an end. Tomorrow, I'm catching a chopper, and will deliver 5 Christmas trees and several bags of goodies to the 4th Infantry Battalion. I intend to visit Alpha Co. (Ken's old unit) and distribute the gifts there in his memory. I love you, Bette

December 20, 1970

It's now 10.45 p.m. and I'm waiting on about eight guys to finish calling home. It's nice and quiet so I decided to write a few lines.

My trip up to North English was overshadowed by a very sad incident. I took four beautiful, live Christmas trees, to distribute at Alpha Co. We left the trees at N. English so I could drop in and say hello to Bravo Co. and our chopper was headed back to pick them up. Suddenly, we received a radio call that a GI was missing from the beach. This was the CO's chopper, and he was aboard, so we headed straight for the beach and began looking out over the ocean. Then we got word that two guys were missing.

Our chopper landed on the beach, dropped off me, and a couple officers, and loaded on several guys to help in the rescue. There were about seven GI's on the whole beach. One had been swimming with two others and made it back, while they got caught in a current.

While sitting on the beach in the warm sand, someone yelled out, "there he is" and started stripping and running out in the water. I watched, as waves carried the body in, and then as several guys brought him to shore. They tried to revive him but couldn't.

I can't tell you how numb I felt, as I sat there and watched. I experienced no emotion – no anything. I just imagined how his family was going to feel – and right before Christmas. When I left they still hadn't found the other GI. I'll always picture that bare beach lined with steel pots, and field gear. When the chopper returned after taking him away, and we began to lift off, I glanced at the floor and noticed fresh pine needles from four lovely Christmas trees. It had started out as such a beautiful Friday afternoon...

Well, I better go upstairs and check on those phone calls. Oh, also today, we had a handshake tour – Johnny Grant and five of his starlets. Love, Bette

December 28, 1970

Well, the big day is over and all that remains is taking down the trimmings. We had an unusual and interesting Christmas. Several weeks ago I had a brainstorm, and thought that since most GI's go home and never get a chance to see the Vietnamese culture, it would be good for them to learn about Christmas in Vietnam.

This resulted in our providing a "Vietnamese Christmas Buffet". Our cooks prepared a typical festive meal, and the staff were there to serve it while explaining to the guys what they were eating. Alice, Gerry, and I wore our ao dais, and it was the first time most of the GI's had ever seen them on American women.

Christmas Eve, the three of us were invited to the home of our interpreter and staff supervisor for a holiday Vietnamese dinner. The little modest house that her husband built was decorated beautifully, and several Vietnamese/American couples were also invited. It was a marvelous experience of sharing each other's customs. We had a shrimp and pork roll, boiled beef, raw fish (which I didn't try), noodles, and salad. They also served Cold Duck wine, which was delicious.

Later that evening at the USO, there were very few guys, but I popped some popcorn while everyone sat around playing cards. Someone even played a guitar and sang.

Christmas night, our interpreter invited, Gerry, plus a friend and I, to see their Catholic Church that was all lit up. We were converged on by a group of children who viewed us with great curiosity.

I still haven't written to anyone concerning a new job with USO. I would like to see how I feel when I get home. Maybe I'll be ready to cross the sea again, or maybe I'd be ready for a stateside job. Who knows?

Well, I've got to get busy and plan next months activities. The guys across the street just said to tell you again how good the cookies and candy are with a glass of milk...

*One of the first people I met in Qui Nhon was a lovely Vietnamese
woman on the USO staff who served as our interpreter and liaison for
problem solving. She explained how she and her family fled North Vietnam
from the communists. Her family and others had formed a small Catholic
community in Qui Nhon where they could maintain their religious beliefs.
As she described how they had to leave everything dear to them, including
their dog, and only take what could be carried onto the boat, it seemed to
fit into the portrayal of what our government referred to as the "domino
effect" and people desiring self-determination. Accounts since then of our
involvement in that conflict are beyond the scope of what I choose to sort
out, but all these years since our withdrawal from Vietnam I have longed
for the safety of my friend and her family.*

January 9, 1971

Mom, I sure was sorry I didn't reach you on your birthday, but the main
thing is you knew I was thinking about you. The big piece of news this
week is that everyone in the Qui Nhon area and for miles around is just
a bit more appreciative of each new day. Wednesday night about 2:15am
we were all shaken out of a sound sleep by a horrifying explosion. My
eyes opened just in time to see one of the wall panels next to my bed come
ripping out at the ceiling. The bed caught it so I wasn't hit. I yelled at
Gerry to take cover due to the fact that my wall was falling in. Ha! I drug
the mattress off my bed, and pulled it over me as I made it to the floor.
I was quickly joined by, Alice, from the next room. We waited for more
explosions, but everything was eerily quiet until we got up to hear people
opening their doors to see what had happened. All the men were of course
in full combat gear, and there we stood in our pajamas, (I soon wrapped
up in a poncho liner). Then, all of a sudden the real fireworks began from
the other side of a small mountain, not far away. The whole sky lit up, a
mushroom type cloud formed, and explosions went off, one right after the
other, like you just wouldn't believe. The officers had in the meantime
called in, and found out it was the ARVN ammunitions storage dump that
had been hit. We stood outside my door and watched this from 2:15 a.m.
until about 4:00 a.m., and it was still going as strong as when it first began,
so we decided to go back to bed. My wall was still hanging there, so it
was rather cold, and you'll be glad to know I wore my furry slippers for
the rest of the night. About 4:30 a.m., another terrific explosion shook the
whole compound again, and on and on after that until after 7:00a.m. The
worst thing that happened in our immediate area, were mirrors falling off
walls, etc., but about nine people, mostly Koreans, were wounded badly

and some killed at the site.

Visiting with people the next day, it seems that everyone for miles around thought it had hit them directly. They say it had the same strength as, I think, 12 tons of T&T. If it hadn't been for that little mountain, we would have felt it much worse. That was more than enough excitement to last me till I go home. Some of the guys made tapes of the blasts, and you'd think it was the end of the world.

Tuesday, I went down to Cam Ranh Bay to visit Mary. I flew in an Otter, on a currier flight that went to Phu Cat, Pleiku, Na Trang, Dong Ba Tinm, and on to Cam Ranh. Mary is quite unhappy since she has come back on her second tour, so she is being transferred down in the Delta to Binh Thuy. I really think that one eighteen- month tour over here is enough for everyone. Anyway, Mary and I had a nice visit. Two Air Force colonels took us out to dinner. The next day, we drove all over the base, in addition to some of the small surrounding towns. The girls in Cam Ranh have lovely trailers to live in, however, there are three girls living in each trailer, and their drive takes about 45 minutes to and from work. That's how large that base is. After seeing how others live, and what their clubs are like, I'm totally satisfied right where I am in Qui Nhon. I feel that once again I've really been lucky.

I haven't written cousin, Marilyn, but I do plan to stop off there to look over the job situation. A lot of young people work near Denver so they can go skiing, and it might be nice to be closer to home than halfway around the world. At this time, I understand USO doesn't have any openings in Europe, so we'll just have to wait and see what happens. I guess I don't have to be in any great hurry. Thank goodness, I have a home and family.

January 16, 1971
Exactly seventeen months ago, I arrived in Saigon. Gee how the time has flown…

The most unusual thing I can tell you about in this episode is my experience on the firing range. Some of the guys let me go with them for target practice. I got to shoot an M-16; M-60 machine-gun; a 45 revolver; and a grenade launcher. There was a whole group of GI's shooting, and my ears haven't been the same since. I even hit the target several times. Ha!

One of them has been asked to head a new drug abuse program. GI's that are on hard drugs can turn themselves in without being reprimanded. He's working with his 2nd patient who has been an addict for over a year, and was a pusher "back in the world".

Sunday! It's another gorgeous day in "Qui Nhon by the Sea". The monsoons are just about over and the lovely weather has arrived. Hopefully I'll come home with a tan. Love you, Bette.

January 22, 1971

What a nice week this has been. Alice and I were invited to take a steak cookout to LZ Beaver, and afterward to dine at the General's Mess at LZ English, Brigade Headquarters for the 173rd Airborne.

We flew up Wednesday, served steaks to 100 GI's, and then had dinner at English, and spent the night. We flew back to Qui Nhon, Thursday morning, in a "Ranger" helicopter. It is a fairly new model and lots of fun. The Ranger is like a little hot rod in the sky. Then yesterday afternoon, Alice told me my assignment was to go home and start on my DEROS tan.

I spoke with, Frazier, last week in Saigon, and he's made my plane reservations. I'll stay one night in Hawaii and the ticket is open from Denver to Oklahoma City. Mr. Shireman, offered me a job in Thailand at a USO, but I turned it down. I think I would eventually like an assignment in Europe. If you read anything about TET, don't worry. We are closing those three days and will take extra precautions. Love, Bette

January 28, 1971

We closed down the USO Club for three days so our Vietnamese staff could be off for TET, and we've been having a lovely time. I sunbathe in the afternoon, and at night I've been invited to my favorite officer's club. It's a small one next to the sea. There is soft music and a candle on each table. Usually, they show a movie about 9 o'clock, and on top of all that, their food is delicious.

Yesterday, Gerry and I went visiting. During the "TET" New Year celebration, the Vietnamese buy new clothes, prepare lots of food, and for three days go from place to place visiting their friends. Yesterday, we went to the home of our dear interpreter, and to visit our mamasans. We ate some kind of rice that was real sticky, bananas with a hot Korean type sauce, delicious sweet onions, and homemade candy.

Our mamasan lives in a refugee camp. All the families there are Catholic, and have left homes elsewhere when the VC moved in. Our mamasan's husband was killed 5 years ago, so she moved to Qui Nhon fearing the VC would return to kill her and her five children. She seemed very pleased that we came to visit.

Yesterday, we watched the Miss Black America Show. Then, I wrapped and mailed home three boxes of my belongings. None of us knew what to expect from "Charlie" this TET, but things have been very quiet. Maybe he's concentrating on Cambodia. What a mess… Don't even ask my opinion of all this, because I just don't know. There certainly isn't an easy answer to any of it.

Well, I guess that's enough gab for now.

19 days!!!!!!!!!! (a real short-timer)!   Much love, Bette

February 8, 1971

Mary called this week, and she is leaving Vietnam to open up a new USO Club in Udorn, Thailand. Our boss offered to look there for an opening for me, but I told him I was ready to leave the orient for a while. I'm sure it will all work out for the best, as it always has.

February 9, 1971

Alice learned I am eligible to take a leave of absence without pay. If that's the case, maybe I'll just wait for a good USO assignment to show up. Well, it won't be long now. Of course I have very mixed emotions, but I'm getting real anxious to see all of you.

There are lots of things going on over here that you'll be reading about soon. It will be most interesting to
see how it all works out… Love, Bette

Monday February 15, 1971 (a letter from my mother to my grandmother, Mamoo)…

Dearest Mother:

Well, by the time this letter reaches you, our Bette should be on her way home! I surely am glad that she didn't sign up again for over there. She has enjoyed it so much, but I'm sure other places would be just as interesting, and a change would be good for her.

Spent another quiet Sunday. There's really not much to do to get ready for Bette's return. The house is still nice and tidy. It's another beautiful Oklahoma day. I wonder if our spring weather will be cool and stormy. It's been so dry here.

Think of you much and love you dearly, Violet

EPILOGUE

In the months following my return from Vietnam, there were some rough patches along the way. While working at a part-time job in Denver, I struggled in an effort to fit back into life in America. This resulted in the decision to drive all night through a frightening thunderstorm, making my way back to family in Oklahoma, City. When I arrived, I found that my cousin Dick and his wife Vicki had also moved back home to start a small business. This was not surprising, because even as adults my cousins and I had always been welcome to find comfort, support, and shelter at home.

Since all of the bedrooms were occupied, I found peaceful sanctuary in a walk-in closet. All I needed was a mattress on the floor and a small stool on which to set a light for reading. This was a perfect arrangement for about three months while I attempted to work through the cultural shock of being back in the states. I also felt somewhat invisible because no one asked or probably knew what to ask about the role I played during the war.

As fate would have it, I was thrown a lifeline when the USO offered me another position at the Club in Victorville, California, working with military personnel stationed at George Air Force Base. Nine months later while attending a USO conference in New York City, I was surprised to check into the hotel and find a message for me at the front desk from Mary McGlasson. It read: "I'm in a room down the hall, and want to know if you would like to join me in opening a new USO Center in Hanau, Germany?"

Of course I was thrilled, and soon found myself serving a three-year tour in Europe. In some respects, events during that period in the mid 1970's, were more challenging to me personally than they had been in Vietnam. By then I was hoping to find a relationship I could make a commitment to long-term, but that possibility kept eluding me. The military was dealing with complex problems of drug abuse and racial tension that had a stressful affect on our work, plus our staff strived to be culturally sensitive regarding how we provided programs extending into the small German community. Becoming a tour guide, supervising the Club, driving troops to ancient castles was wonderful, but there were many times that I was once again pulled out of my comfort zone. That, however, is a story of its own.

Finally, after traveling down many more highways and byways, I returned to Oklahoma, and in my mid 40's met my wonderful husband, Richard. We have been married now for almost 30 years, have lived in four states, provided care for family elders, and adopted many stray dogs and cats.

In re-visiting this period of my life to write a memoir, I feel that the process itself has been surprisingly therapeutic. My hope is that sharing my experiences in Vietnam will reach those who might benefit from it in ways I can't imagine. Perhaps seeing someone in a picture, or recognizing a familiar scene could bring about a moment of healing or pleasant reflection. It feels rather like sending a message out in a bottle and watching the waves carry it to places and people unknown. That seems to be a fitting metaphor for how things in this account have unfolded. Certainly in my wildest dreams, I could not have visualized the mysterious blossoming of such an interesting life.

ABOUT THE AUTHOR

Bette and her husband, Richard, live in the "Land of Enchantment", Albuquerque, New Mexico and wish everyone the health, harmony, and wholeness we all deserve.

bettequinhonuso@gmail.com

Bette with her letters from Qui Nhon

Made in the USA
Coppell, TX
26 May 2024

32820037R10075